# *English Grammar and Common Errors*

# English Grammar and Common Errors

Dr. Joginder Paul
*Govt. Mohindera College*
*Patiala. Punjab*

**Cyber Tech Publications**
4264/3, Ansari Road, Darya Ganj
New Delhi-110002 (India)
Phones : 23244078/43559448
E-mail : cybertechpublications@gmail.com

ENGLISH GRAMMAR AND COMMON ERRORS



First Published 2015
ISBN : 978-93-5053-435-9
Price: 900/-

Page: 240



*Published in India by*

CYBER TECH PUBLICATIONS
4264/3, Ansari Road, Darya Ganj
New Delhi-110002 (India)
Phones : 23244078/43559448
E-mail : cybertechpublications@gmail.com
Visit us at www.cybertechpublication.com

---

*Printed at* : Asian Offset Press Delhi

# Preface

In linguistics, grammar is the set of structural rules governing the composition of clauses, phrases, and words in any given natural language. The term refers also to the study of such rules, and this field includes morphology, syntax, and phonology, often complemented by phonetics, semantics, and pragmatics.

The term grammar is often used by non-linguists with a very broad meaning. As Jeremy Butterfield puts it, "Grammar is often a generic way of referring to any aspect of English that people object to." However, linguists use it in a much more specific sense. Speakers of a language have a set of internalised rules for using that language. This is grammar, and the vast majority of the information in it is acquired-at least in the case of one's native language-not by conscious study or instruction, but by observing other speakers; much of this work is done during infancy. Learning a language later in life usually involves a greater degree of explicit instruction.

The term "grammar" can also be used to describe the rules that govern the linguistic behaviour of a group of speakers. The term "English grammar", therefore, may have several meanings. It may refer to the whole of English grammar, that is, to the grammars of all the speakers of the language, in which case, the term encompasses a great deal of variation. Alternatively, it may refer only to what is common to the grammars of all. or of the vast majority of English speakers (such as subject-verb-object word order in simple declarative sentences). Or it may refer to the rules of a particular, relatively well-defined variety of English.

**—Author**

# Contents

*Preface* *v*
1. Active or Passive Voice 1
2. Adjectives 29
3. Adverbs 50
4. Articles 66
5. Auxiliary Verbs 84
6. Conditionals 99
7. Conjunctions 119
8. Determiners 141
9. Idioms and Interjections 155
10. Nouns 171
11. Phrases 186
12. Clauses 203
13. Tenses 219
*Bibliography* 231

Chapter-1

# Active or Passive Voice

## VOICE (GRAMMAR)

In grammar, the voice (also called diathesis and (rarely) gender (of verbs)) of a verb describes the relationship between the action (or state) that the verb expresses and the participants identified by its arguments (subject, object, etc.). When the subject is the agent or doer of the action, the verb is in the active voice. When the subject is the patient, target or undergoer of the action, the verb is said to be in the passive voice.

For example, in the sentence:

The

cat

*ate the mouse.*

The verb "ate" is in the active voice, but in the sentence:

*The mouse was eaten by the cat.*

The verbal phrase "was eaten" is passive.

In

*The hunter killed the bear.*

The verb "killed" is in the active voice, and the doer of the action is the "hunter". To make this passive:

*The bear was killed by the hunter.*

The verbal phrase "was killed" is followed by the word "by" and then by the doer "hunter".

In a transformation from an active-voice clause to an equivalent passive-voice construction, the subject and the direct object switch grammatical roles. The direct object gets *promoted* to subject, and the subject *demoted* to an (optional)complement. In the examples above, *the mouse* serves as the direct object in the active-voice version, but becomes the subject in the passive version. The subject of the active-voice version, *the cat*, becomes part of a prepositional phrase in the passive version of the sentence, and could be left out entirely.

## HISTORY

In the traditional grammar of Ancient Greek, voice was called diáthesis "arrangement" or "condition", with three subcategories: active enérgeia, passive páthos, middle mesótçs. In Latin there are 5 voices (Latin: genera verborum, sg. genus verbi): active, passive, neuter, common and deponent (Latin: [genus] activum, passivum, neutrum, commune, deponens).

### Active

The active voice is the most commonly used in many languages and represents the "normal" case, in which the subject of the verb is the agent.

In the active voice the subject of the sentence performs the action or causes the happening denoted by the verb.

### Passive

The passive voice is employed in a clause whose subject expresses the theme or patient of the verb. That is, it undergoes an action or has its state changed.

In the passive voice the grammatical subject of the verb is the recipient (not the doer) of the action denoted by the verb.

The Spanish language and the English language use a *periphrastic* passive voice; that is, it is not a single word form, but rather a construction making use of other word forms. Specifically, it is made up of a form of the auxiliary verb *to be* and a past participle of the main verb. In other languages, such as Latin, the passive voice is simply marked on the verb byinflection: *librum legit*"He reads the book"; *liber legitur*"The book is read".

## Middle

Some languages (such as Albanian, Bengali, Fula, Tamil, Sanskrit, Icelandic, Swedish and Ancient Greek) have a **middle voice**. This is a set of inflections or constructions which is to some extent different from both the active and passive voices. The middle voice is said to be in the middle between the active and the passive voices because the subject often cannot be categorized as either agent or patient but may have elements of both. For example it may express what would be an intransitive verb in English. For example, in *The casserole cooked in the oven, cooked* is syntactically active butsemantically passive. In Classical Greek, the middle voice often has a reflexive sense: the subject acts on or for itself, such as "The boy washes himself", or "The boy washes". It can be transitive or intransitive. It can occasionally be used in a causative sense, such as "The father causes his son to be set free", or "The father ransoms his son".

In English there is no verb form for the middle voice, though some uses may be classified as middle voice, often resolved via a reflexive pronoun, as in "Fred shaved", which may be expanded to "Fred shaved himself" – contrast with active "Fred shaved John" or passive "John was shaved by Fred". This need not be reflexive, as in "my clothes soaked in detergent overnight". English used to have a distinct form, called the passival, which was displaced over the early 19th century by thepassive progressive (progressive passive), and is no longer used in English. In the passival, one would say "the house is building", which is today instead "the house is being built"; likewise "the meal is eating", which is now "the meal is being eaten". Note that the similar "Fred is shaving" and "the clothes are soaking" remain grammatical. It is suggested that the progressive passive was popularized by the Romantic poets, and is connected with Bristol usage.

Many deponent verbs in Latin are survivals of the Proto-Indo-European middle voice.

## Others

Some languages have even more grammatical voices. For example, Classical Mongolian features five voices: active, passive, causative, reciprocal, and cooperative. Hebrew has active, passive, causative, intensive and reflexive voices.

The antipassive voice deletes or demotes the object of transitive verbs, and promotes the actor to an intransitive subject. This voice is very common among ergative–absolutive languages (which may feature passive voices as well), but also occurs among nominative–accusative languages.

There are also constructions in some languages that appear to change the valence of a verb, but in fact do not. So called hierarchical or inversion languages are of this sort. Their agreement system will be sensitive to an external person or animacy hierarchy (or a combination of both): 1 > 2 > 3 or Anim > Inan and so forth. E. g., in Meskwaki (an Algonquian language), verbs inflect for both subject and object, but agreement markers do not have inherent values for these. Rather, a third marker, the direct or inverse marker, indicates the proper interpretation: *ne-wa:pam-e:-w-a* [1-look. at-DIR-3-3Sg] "I am looking at him", but *ne-wa:pam-ekw-w-a* [1-look. at-INV-3-3Sg] "He is looking at me". Some scholars (notably Rhodes) have analyzed this as a kind of obligatory passivization dependent on animacy, while others have claimed it is not a voice at all, but rather see inversion as another type of alignment, parallel to nominative–accusative ergative–absolutive, split-S, and fluid-S alignments.

## Passive in topic-prominent languages

Topic-prominent languages like Mandarin tend not to employ the passive voice as frequently. Mandarin-speakers construct the passive voice by using the coverb «ˆ (*bèi*) and rearranging the usual word order. For example, this sentence using active voice:

## Fourth person in Finnic languages

Some languages do not contrast voices, but have other interesting constructions similar to this. For example, Finnic languages such as Finnish and Estonian have a "passive", expressed by conjugating the verb in "common person". Although it is generally referred to as the passive ("*passiivi*") in Finnish grammars, it may more appropriately be referred to as the fourth-person form of a verb.

The function of the fourth person is simply to leave out the agent. The agent is almost always human and never mentioned. The grammatical role of the object remains unaltered, and thus transitivity may also be used. For example, the fourth-person construction *Ikkuna hajotettiin*, with a transitive verb, means "Someone broke the window", while the third-person construction *Ikkuna hajosi* uses the anticausative and means "The window broke".

## Impersonal in Celtic languages

Celtic languages possess an inflection commonly called the "impersonal" or "autonomous" form, of similar origin to the Latin "passive-impersonal". This is similar to a passive construction in that the agent of the verb is not specified. However its syntax is different from prototypical passives, in that the object of the action remains in the accusative.

It is similar to the use of the pronoun "*on*" in French. It increasingly corresponds to the passive in modern English, in which there is a trend towards avoiding the use of the passive unless it is specifically required to omit the subject. It also appears to be similar to the "fourth person" mentioned in the preceding paragraph.

The construction has equal validity in transitive and intransitive clauses, and the best translation into English is normally by using the "dummy" subjects "they", "one", or impersonal "you". For example, the common sign against tobaccoconsumption has its closest direct translation in English as "No smoking":

| Ná | caitear | tabac |
|---|---|---|
| Don't | use-impersonal | tobacco. |

An example of its use as an intransitive is:

| Téithear | go dtí | an sráidbhaile | go minic | Dé Sathairn |
|---|---|---|---|---|
| Go-imper-sonal | to | the village | often | Saturday |

"People often go to the village of a Saturday."

The difference between the autonomous and a true passive is that while the autonomous focuses on the action and overtly avoids mentioning the actor, there is nonetheless an anonymous agent who may be referred to in the sentence. For instance

| Théití | ag ithe | béile | le chéile |
|---|---|---|---|
| go [PAST-HABIT-AUT] | eat [PROG] | meal | with each other |
| People used to go | eating | a meal | together |

In English, the formation of the passive allows the optional inclusion of an agent in a prepositional phrase, "by the man", etc. Where English would leave out the noun phrase, Irish uses the autonomous; where English includes the noun phrase, Irish uses its periphrastic passive - which can also leave out the noun phrase:

The tobacco was smoked (by the man)

| Bhí | an tabac | caite | (ag an bhfear) |
|---|---|---|---|
| Was | the tobacco | consumed | (by the man) |

The impersonal endings have been re-analysed as a passive voice in Modern Welsh and the agent can be included after the preposition *gan* (*by*):

*Cenir y gân gan y côr.*

The song is sung by the choir.

Dynamic and static passive

Some languages draw a distinction between static (or stative) passive voice, and dynamic (or eventive) passive voice. Examples include English, German, Swedish, Spanish and Italian. "Static" means that an action was done to the subject at a certain point in time resulting in a state in the time focussed upon, whereas "dynamic" means that an action takes place.

## German

Static passive auxiliary verb: **sein**

Dynamic passive auxiliary verb: **werden**

*Der Rasen ist gemäht* ("The lawn is mown", static)

*Der Rasen wird gemäht* ("The lawn is being mown", literally "The lawn becomes mown", dynamic)

## English

Static passive auxiliary verb: **be** (the "be-passive") Dynamic passive auxiliary verb: **get** (the "get-passive")

Note that for some speakers of English this is not accepted and is considered colloquial or sub-standard.

*The grass is cut* (static)

*The grass gets cut* or *The grass is being cut* (dynamic)

## Swedish

Static passive auxiliary verb: **vara** (är, var, varit)

Dynamic passive auxiliary verb: **bli** (blir, blev, blivit) Dynamic passive in Swedish is also frequently expressed with the s-ending.

*Dörren är öppnad.*"The door has been opened."

*Dörren blir öppnad.*"The door is being opened."

The **vara** passive is often synonymous with, and sometimes preferable to, simply using the corresponding adjective:

*Dörren är öppen.*"The door is open."

The **bli** passive is often synonymous with, and sometimes preferable to, the s-passive:

*Dörren öppnas.*"The door is opening."

## Spanish

Spanish has two verbs corresponding to English *to be*: *ser* and *estar*. *Ser* is used to form the ordinary (dynamic) passive voice:

*La puerta es abierta.*"The door is [being] opened [by someone]."

*La puerta es cerrada.*"The door is [being] closed [by someone]."

(Note that this construction is very unidiomatic in this case. The usual phrasing would be *La puerta se cierra.*) *Estar* is used to form what might be termed a static passive voice (not regarded as a passive voice in traditional Spanish grammar):

*La puerta* ***está*** *abierta.*"The door is open.", i. e. it has been opened.

*La puerta* ***está*** *cerrada.*"The door is closed.", i. e. it has been closed.

In both cases, the verb's participle is used as the complement (as is sometimes the case in English).

## Italian

Italian uses two verbs (*essere* and *venire*) to translate the static and the dynamic passive:

Dynamic passive auxiliary verb: **essere** and **venire** (**to be** and **to come**)

*La porta è aperta.* or *La porta* ***viene*** *aperta.* "The door is opened [by someone]" or "The door **comes** open [by someone]".

*La porta è chiusa.* or *La porta* ***viene*** *chiusa.* "The door is closed [by someone]" or "The door **comes** closed [by someone]".

Static passive auxiliary verb: **essere** (to be)

*La porta è aperta.* "The door is open," i. e. it has been opened.

*La porta è chiusa.*"The door is closed," i. e. it has been closed.

## Venetian

In Venetian (Vèneto) the difference between dynamic (true) passive and stative (adjectival) passive is more clear cut, using**ĕser** (to be) only for the static passives and **vegner** (to become, to come) only for the dynamic passive:

*£a porta* ***³a vien*** *verta.* "The door is opened", dynamic

*£a porta* ***³a xè / l'è*** *verta.* "The door is open", static

Static forms represents much more a property or general condition, whereas the dynamic form is a real passive action entailing "by someone":

***èser*** *proteto.* "To be protected = to be in a safe condition", static

***vegner*** *proteto*. "To be protected = to be defended (by so)", dynamic

***èser*** *considarà*. "To be considered = to have a (good) reputation", static

***vegner*** *considarà*. "To be taken into consideration (by people, by so)", dynamic

***èser*** *raprexentà (a l'ONU)*. "To be represented (at the UN) = to have a representation", static

***vegner*** *raprexentà a l'ONU (da un de³egà)*. "To be represented at the UN (by a delegate)", dynamic

## PASSIVE AND ACTIVE VOICES

Verbs are also said to be either *active* (The executive committee approved the new policy) or *passive* (The new policy was approved by the executive committee) in voice. In the active voice, the subject and verb relationship is straightforward: the subject is a be-er or a do-er and the verb moves the sentence along. In the **passive voice**, the subject of the sentence is neither a do-er or a be-er, but is acted upon by some other **agent** or by something unnamed (The new policy was approved). Computerized grammar checkers can pick out a passive voice construction from miles away and ask you to revise it to a more active construction. There is nothing inherently wrong with the passive voice, but if you can say the same thing in the active mode, do so. Your text will have more pizzazz as a result, since passive verb constructions tend to lie about in their pajamas and avoid actual work.

We find an overabundance of the passive voice in sentences created by self-protective business interests, magniloquent educators, and bombastic military writers (who must get weary of

this accusation), who use the passive voice to avoid responsibility for actions taken. Thus "Cigarette ads were designed to appeal especially to children" places the burden on the ads — as opposed to "We designed the cigarette ads to appeal especially to children," in which "we" accepts responsibility. At a White House press briefing we might hear that "The President was advised that certain members of Congress were being audited" rather than "The Head of the Internal Revenue service advised the President that her agency was auditing certain members of Congress" because the passive construction avoids responsibility for advising and for auditing. One further caution about the passive voice: we should not mix active and passive constructions in the same sentence: "The executive committee approved the new policy, and the calendar for next year's meetings was revised" should be recast as "The executive committee approved the new policy and revised the calendar for next year's meeting."

Take the quiz (below) as an exercise in recognizing and changing passive verbs.

The passive voice does exist for a reason, however, and its presence is not always to be despised. The passive is particularly useful (even recommended) in two situations:

- *When it is more important to draw our attention to the person or thing acted upon:* The unidentified victim was apparently struck during the early morning hours.
- *When the actor in the situation is not important:* The aurora borealis can be observed in the early morning hours.

The passive voice is especially helpful (and even regarded as mandatory) in scientific or technical writing or lab reports, where the actor is not really important but the process or principle being described is of ultimate importance. Instead of writing "I poured 20 cc of acid into the beaker," we would write "Twenty cc of acid is/was poured into the beaker." The passive voice is also useful when describing, say, a mechanical process in which the details of process are much more important than anyone's taking responsibility for the action: "The first coat of primer paint is applied immediately after the acid rinse."

We use the passive voice to good effect in a paragraph in which we wish to shift emphasis from what was the object in a first sentence to what becomes the subject in subsequent sentences.

The executive committee approved an entirely new policy for dealing with academic suspension and withdrawal. The policyhad been written by a subcommittee on student behavior. If students withdraw from course work before suspension can take effect, the policy states, a mark of "IW"....

The paragraph is clearly about this new policy so it is appropriate that *policy* move from being the object in the first sentence to being the subject of the second sentence. The passive voice allows for this transition.

### Verbals in Passive Structures

**Verbals or verb forms** can also take on features of the passive voice. An **infinitive phrase in the passive voice**, for instance, can perform various functions within a sentence (just like the active forms of the infinitive).

- Subject: To be elected by my peers is a great honor.
- Object: That child really likes to be read to by her mother.
- Modifier: Grasso was the first woman to be elected governor in her own right.

The same is true of **passive gerunds**.

- Subject: Being elected by my peers was a great thrill.
- Object: I really don't like being lectured to by my boss.
- Object of preposition: I am so tired of being lectured to by my boss.

With **passive participles**, part of the passive construction is often omitted, the result being a simple modifying **participial phrase**.

- [~~Having been~~] designed for off-road performance, the Pathseeker does not always behave well on paved highways.

## ACTIVE VOICE

**Active voice** is a grammatical voice common in many of the world's languages. It is the unmarked voice for clauses featuring a transitive verb in nominative–accusative languages, including English and most other Indo-European languages.

Active voice is used in a clause whose subject expresses the agent of the main verb. That is, the subject does the action designated by the verb. A sentence whose agent is marked as grammatical subject is called an active sentence. In contrast, a sentence in which the subject has the role of patient or theme is named a passive sentence, and its verb is expressed in passive voice. Many languages have both an active and a passive voice; this allows for greater flexibility in sentence construction, as either the semantic agent or patient may take the syntactic role of subject.

## English passive voice

The passive voice is a grammatical construction (specifically, a"voice"). The noun or noun phrase that would be the object of an active sentence (such as *Our troops defeated the enemy*) appears as the subject of a sentence with passive voice (e. g. *The enemy was defeated by our troops*).

The subject of a sentence or clause featuring the passive voice typically denotes the recipient of the action (the patient) rather than the performer (the agent). The passive voice in English is formed periphrastically: the usual form uses the auxiliary verb *be* (or*get*) together with the past participle of the main verb.

For example, *Caesar was stabbed by Brutus* uses the passive voice. The subject denotes the person (Caesar) affected by the action of the verb. The agent is expressed here with the phrase *by Brutus*, but this can be omitted. The equivalent sentence inactive voice is *Brutus stabbed Caesar*, in which the subject denotes the doer, or agent, Brutus. A sentence featuring the passive voice is sometimes called a *passive sentence*, and a verb phrase in passive voice is sometimes called a *passive verb*.

English allows a number of passive constructions which are not possible in many of the other languages with similar passive formation. These include promotion of an indirect object to subject (as in *Tom was given a bag*) and promotion of the complement of apreposition (as in *Sue was operated on*, leaving a stranded preposition).

Use of the English passive varies with writing style and field. Some publications' style sheets discourage use of the passive voice, while others encourage it. Although some purveyors of usage advice, including George Orwell and William Strunk, Jr. and E. B. White discourage use of the passive in English, its usefulness is generally recognized, particularly in cases where the patient is more important than the agent, but also in some cases where it is desired to emphasize the agent.

## Identifying the English passive

The passive voice is a specific grammatical construction; not every expression that serves to take focus away from the performer of an action is classified as an instance of passive voice. The essential components of the English passive voice are a form of the auxiliary verb *be* (or sometimes *get*), and the past participle of the main verb denoting the action. For example:

... that all men **are created** equal...

We **have been** cruelly **deceived**.

The captain **was struck** by a missile.

I **got kicked** in the face during the fight.

(For exceptions, see Additional passive constructions below.) The agent (the doer of the action) may be specified, using aprepositional phrase with the preposition *by*, as in the third example, but it is equally possible to omit this, as is done in the other examples.

A distinction is made between the above type of clause, and those of similar form in which the past participle is used as an ordinary adjective, and the verb *be* or similar is simply a copula linking the subject of the sentence to that adjective. For example:

I am **excited** (right now).

This would not normally be classed as a passive sentence, since the participle *excited* is used adjectivally to denote a state, not to denote an action of excitation (as it would in the passive *the electron was excited with a laser pulse*). SeeStative and adjectival uses below.

Sentences which do not follow the pattern described above are not considered to be in the passive voice, even if they have a similar function of avoiding or marginalizing reference to the agent. An example is the sentence *A stabbing occurred*, where mention of the stabber is avoided, but the sentence is nonetheless cast in the active voice, with the verbal noun*stabbing* forming the subject of the simple past tense of the verb *occur*. (Similarly *There was a stabbing*.) Occasionally, however, writers misapply the term "passive voice" to sentences of this type. An example of this loose usage can be found in the following extract from an article from *The New Yorker* about Bernard Madoff (bolding and italics added; bold text indicates the verbs misidentified as passive voice):

Two sentences later, Madoff said, "When I began the Ponzi scheme, I believed it **would end** shortly, and I would be able to extricate myself, and my clients, from the scheme." As he read this, he betrayed no sense of how absurd it was *to use the passive voice* in regard to his scheme, as if it were a spell of bad weather that had descended on him... In most of the rest of the statement, one not only heard *the aggrieved passive voice*, but felt the hand of a lawyer: "To the best of my recollection, my fraud **began** in the early nineteen-nineties." The intransitive verbs *would end* and *began* are in fact in the active voice. Although the speaker uses the words in a manner that subtly diverts responsibility from him, this is not accomplished by use of passive voice.

## Reasons for using the passive voice

The passive voice can be used without referring to the agent of an action; it may therefore be used when the agent is unknown or unimportant, or the speaker does not wish to mention the agent.

- Three stores were robbed last night. (the identity of the agent may be unknown)
- A new cancer drug has been discovered. (the identity of the agent may be unimportant in the context)
- Mistakes have been made on this project. (the speaker may not wish to identify the agent)

The last sentence illustrates a frequently criticized use of the passive – the evasion of responsibility by failure to mention the agent (which may even be the speaker himself).

Agentless passives are common in scientific writing, where the agent may be irrelevant:

- The mixture was heated to 300°C.

However the passive voice can also be used together with a mention of the agent, using a *by*-phrase. In this case the reason for use of the passive is often connected with the positioning of this phrase at the end of the clause (unlike in the active voice, where the agent, as subject, normally precedes the verb). Here, in contrast to the examples above, passive constructions may in fact serve to place emphasis on the agent, since it is natural for information being emphasized to come at the end:

- Don't you see? The patient was murdered **by his own doctor**!

In more technical terms, such uses can be expected in sentences where the agent is the focus (*comment, rheme*), while the patient (the undergoer of the action) is the *topic* or *theme* There is a tendency for sentences to be formulated so as to place the focus at the end, and this can motivate the choice of active or passive voice:

- My taxi hit an old lady. (the taxi is the topic, the lady is the focus)
- My mother was hit by a taxi. (the mother is the topic, the taxi is the focus)

Similarly, the passive may be used because the noun phrase denoting the agent is a long one (containing many modifiers), since it is convenient to place such phrases at the end of a clause:

- The breakthrough was achieved by Burlingame and Evans, two researchers in the university's genetic engineering lab.

In some situations, the passive may be used so that the most dramatic word, or punchline, appears at the end of the sentence.

## STYLE ADVICE

### Advice against the passive voice

Many language critics and language-usage manuals discourage use of the passive voice. This advice is not usually found in older guides, emerging only in the first half of the twentieth century. In 1916, the British writer Arthur Quiller-Couch criticized this grammatical voice:

Generally, use transitive verbs, that strike their object; and use them in the active voice, eschewing the stationary passive, with its little auxiliary *its's* and *was's*, and its participles getting into the light of your adjectives, which should be few. For, as a rough law, by his use of the straight verb and by his economy of adjectives you can tell a man's style, if it be masculine or neuter, writing or 'composition'.

Two years later, in the original 1918 edition of *The Elements of Style*, Cornell University Professor of English William Strunk, Jr. warned against excessive use of the passive voice:

The active voice is usually more direct and vigorous than the passive... This rule does not, of course, mean that the writer should entirely discard the passive voice, which is frequently convenient and sometimes necessary... The need to make a particular word the subject of the sentence will often... determine which voice is to be used. The habitual use of the active voice, however, makes for forcible writing. This is true not only in narrative concerned principally with action, but in writing of any kind. Many a tame sentence of description or exposition can be made lively and emphatic by substituting a transitive in the active voice for some such perfunctory expression as *there is* or *could be heard*.

In 1926, in the authoritative *A Dictionary of Modern English Usage* (1926), Henry Watson Fowler recommended against transforming active voice forms into passive voice forms, because doing so "... sometimes leads to bad grammar, falseidiom, or clumsiness."

In 1946, in the essay *Politics and the English Language*, George Orwell recommended the active voice as an elementary principle of composition: "Never use the passive where you can use the active."

*The Columbia Guide to Standard American English* (1993) stated that:

*Active voice* makes subjects do something (to something); *passive voice* permits subjects to have something done to them (by someone or something). Some argue that *active voice* is more muscular, direct, and succinct, *passive voice* flabbier, more indirect, and wordier. If you want your words to seem impersonal, indirect, and noncommittal, *passive* is the choice, but otherwise, *active voice* is almost invariably likely to prove more effective.

The principal criticism against the passive voice is its potential for evasion of responsibility. This is because a passive clause may be used to omit the agent even where it is important:

- We had hoped to report on this problem, but the data were inadvertently deleted from our files.

Krista Ratcliffe, a professor at Marquette University, notes the use of passives as an example of the role of grammar as "... a link between words and magical conjuring [... ]: passive voice mystifies accountability by erasing who or what performs an action [... ]."

### Advice in favor of the passive voice

Jan Freeman, a reporter for *The Boston Globe*, said that the passive voice does have its uses, and that "all good writers use the passive voice." For example, despite Orwell's advice to avoid the passive, his *Politics and the English Language*(1946) employs passive voice for about 20 percent of its constructions. By comparison, a statistical study found about 13 percent passive constructions in newspapers and magazines.

Passive writing is not necessarily slack and indirect. Many famously vigorous passages use the passive voice, as in these examples:

- Every valley shall be exalted, and every mountain and hill shall be made low; and the crooked shall be made straight, and the rough places plain. (King James Bible, Isaiah 40:4)
- Now is the winter of our discontent / Made glorious summer by this sun of York. (*Shakespeare's Richard III*, I. 1, ll. 1–2)
- For of those to whom much is given, much is required. (John F. Kennedy's quotation of Luke 12:48 in his address to the Massachusetts legislature, 9 January 1961.)

- Never in the field of human conflict was so much owed by so many to so few. (Winston Churchill addressing the House of Commons, 20 August 1940.)

*Merriam–Webster's Dictionary of English Usage* (1994) recommends the passive voice when identifying the object (receiver) of the action is more important than the subject (agent), and when the agent is unknown, unimportant, or not worth mentioning:

- The child was struck by the car.
- The store was robbed last night.
- Plows should not be kept in the garage.
- Kennedy was elected president.

Despite criticism that the passive can be used to hide responsibility by omitting the agent, the passive can also be used to emphasize the agent. Writers have preferred placing the agent at the end of a clause or sentence to give it greater emphasis, as in the examples given in the previous section:

- Don't you see? The patient was murdered **by his own doctor**!
- The breakthrough was achieved by Burlingame and Evans, two researchers in the university's genetic engineering lab.

Geoffrey Pullum writes that "The passive is not an undesirable feature limited to bad writing, it's a useful construction often needed for clear expression, and every good writer uses it."

## PASSIVE CONSTRUCTIONS

### Canonical passives

In the most commonly considered type of passive clause, a form of the verb *be* (or sometimes *get*) is used as an auxiliarytogether with the past participle of a transitive verb; that verb is missing its direct object, and the patient of the action (that which would be denoted by the direct object of the verb in an active clause) is denoted instead by the subject of the clause. For example, the active clause:

- John threw the ball.

contains *threw* as a transitive verb with *John* as its subject and *the ball* as its direct object. If we recast the verb in the passive voice (*was thrown*), then *the ball* becomes the subject (it is "promoted" to the subject position) and *John*disappears:

- The ball was thrown.

The original subject (the agent) can optionally be re-inserted using the preposition *by*.

- The ball was thrown **by John.**

The above example uses the verb *be* (in the past tense form *was*) to make the passive. It is often possible to use the verb*get* as an alternative (possibly with slightly different meaning); for example, the active sentence "The ball hit Bob" may be recast in either of the following forms:

- Bob was hit by the ball.
- Bob got hit by the ball.

The auxiliary verb of the passive voice (*be* or *get*) may appear in any combination of tense, aspect and mood, and can also appear in non-finite form (infinitive, participle or gerund). See the article on English verb forms for more information. Notice that this includes use of the verb *be* in progressive aspect, which does not normally occur when *be* is used as a simplecopula. Some examples:

- The food **is being served**. (present progressive passive)
- The stadium **will have been built** by next January. (future perfect passive)
- I **would have got/gotten injured** if I had stayed in my place. (conditional perfect passive with *get*)
- It isn't nice **to be insulted**. (passive infinitive)
- **Having been humiliated**, he left the stage. (passive present participle, perfect aspect)

## Promotion of indirect objects

Unlike some other languages, English also allows passive clauses in which an indirect object, rather than a direct object, is promoted to the subject. For example:

- John gave Mary a book. '! Mary was given a book (by John).

In the active form, *gave* is the verb; *John* is its subject, *Mary* its indirect object, and *a book* its direct object. In the passive forms, the indirect object has been promoted and the direct object has been left in place. (In this respect, English resembles dechticaetiative languages.)

It is normally only the first-appearing object that can be promoted; promotion of the indirect object takes place from a construction in which it precedes the direct object (i. e. where there is no *to* or *for* before the indirect object), whereas promotion of the direct object in such cases takes place from a construction in which the indirect object follows the direct (this time being accompanied by *to* or *for*; see English grammar: Verb phrases). For example:

- John gave Mary a book. '! Mary was given a book. (and not normally: ??A book was given Mary.)
- John gave a book **to** Mary. '! A book was given **to** Mary. (and not: *Mary was given a book to.)

Similar restrictions apply to the prepositional passive, as noted in the following section.

Prepositional passive

It is also possible, in some cases, to promote the object of a preposition. This may be called the **prepositional passive**, or sometimes the **pseudo-passive** (although the latter term can also have other meanings, such as being equivalent to the impersonal passive voice, particularly in descriptions of other languages).

- They talked about the problem. '! The problem was talked about.

In the passive form here, the preposition is "stranded"; that is, it is not followed by an object.

The prepositional passive is common especially in informal English. However some potential uses appear grammatically unacceptable; compare the following examples given by Pullum:

- Someone has slept in this bunk. '! This bunk has been slept in. (fully acceptable)

- Someone has slept above this bunk. '! ??This bunk has been slept above. (barely acceptable)

The second sentence appears unacceptable because sleeping above a bunk does not change its state; the verb phrase*been slept above* does not express a "relevantly important property" of the bunk.

It is not usually possible to promote a prepositional object if the verb also has a direct object; any passive rendering of the sentence must instead promote the direct object. For example:

- Someone has put a child in this bunk. '! *This bunk has been put a child in. (unacceptable)
- Someone has put a child in this bunk. '! A child has been put in this bunk. (acceptable)

Exceptions occur with certain idiomatic combinations of verb+object+preposition, such as *take advantage of*:

- I feel people have taken advantage of me. '! I feel I have been taken advantage of. (acceptable)

Stative and adjectival uses

A type of clause that is similar or identical in form to the passive clauses described above has the past participle used to denote not an action, but a state being the result of an action. For example, the sentence *The window was broken* may have two different meanings:

- The window was broken, *i. e.* Someone or something broke the window. (action, event)
- The window was broken, *i. e.* The window was not intact. (resultant state)

The first sentence is an example of the canonical English passive as described above. However the second case is distinct; such sentences are not always considered to be true passives, since the participle is being used adjectivally; they are sometimes called *false passives*. If they are considered to be passives, they may be called *stative* (or *static*, or*resultative*) passives, since they represent a state or result. By contrast the canonical passives, representing an action or event, may then be called *dynamic* or *eventive* passives.

The ambiguity in such sentences arises because the verb *be* is used in English both as the passive auxiliary and as the ordinary copular verb for linking to predicate adjectives. When *get* is used to form the passive, there is no ambiguity: *The window got broken* cannot have a stative meaning. (For ways in which some other languages make this distinction, seePassive voice: Stative and dynamic passive.) If a distinct adjective exists for the purpose of expressing the state, then the past participle is less likely to be used for that purpose; this is the case with the verb *open*, for which there exists an adjective *open*, so the sentence *The door was opened* more likely refers to the action rather than the state, since in the stative case one could simply say *The door was open*.

Past participles of transitive verbs can also be used as adjectives (as in *a **broken** doll*), and the participles used in the above-mentioned "stative" constructions are often considered to be adjectival (in predicative use). Such constructions may then also be called *adjectival passives* (although they are not normally considered true passives). For example:

- She was relieved to find her car.

Here, *relieved* is an ordinary adjective, though it derives from the past participle of *relieve*. In other sentences that same participle may be used to form the true (dynamic) passive: *He was relieved of duty.*

When the verb being put into the passive voice is a stative verb anyway, the distinctions between uses of the past participle become less clear, since the canonical passive already has a stative meaning. (For example: *People **know** his identity* '!*His identity **is known**.)* However it is sometimes possible to impart a dynamic meaning using *get* as the auxiliary, as in *get known* with the meaning "become known".

## Passive constructions without an exactly corresponding active

Some passive constructions are not derived exactly from a corresponding active construction in the ways described above. This is particularly the case with sentences containing content clauses (usually *that*-clauses). Given a sentence in which the role of direct object is played by such a clause, for example

- They say (that) he cheats.

it is possible to convert this to a passive by promoting the content clause to subject; in this case, however, the clause typically does not change its position in the sentence, and an expletive *it* takes the normal subject position:

- It is said that he cheats.

Another way of forming passives in such cases involves promoting the subject of the content clause to the subject of the main clause, and converting the content clause into a non-finite clause with the *to*-infinitive. This infinitive is marked forgrammatical aspect to correspond to the aspect (or past tense) expressed in the content clause. For example:

- They say that he cheats. '! He is said to cheat.
- They think that I am dying. '! I am thought to be dying.
- They report that she came back / has come back. '! She is reported to have come back.
- They say that she will resign. '! *e. g.* She is said to be going to resign.

Some verbs are used almost exclusively in the passive voice. This is the case with *rumor*, for example. The following passive sentences are possible:

- He was rumored to be a war veteran. / It was rumored that he was a war veteran.

but it is not possible to use the active counterpart **They rumored that he was a war veteran.* (This was once possible, but has fallen out of use.)

Another situation in which the passive uses a different construction than the active involves the verb *make*, meaning "compel". When this verb is used in the active voice it takes the bare infinitive (without the particle *to*), but in the passive voice it takes the *to*-infinitive. For example:

- They made Jane attend classes.
- Jane was made **to** attend classes.

## Double passives

The construction called **double passive** can arise when one verb appears in the *to*-infinitive as the complement of another verb.

If the first verb takes a direct object ahead of the infinitive complement (this applies to raising-to-object verbs, where the expected subject of the second verb is raised to the position of object of the first verb), then the passive voice may be used independently for either or both of the verbs:

- We expect you to complete the project. (*you* is raised from subject of *complete* to object of *expect*)
- You **are expected** to complete the project. (passive voice used for *expect*)
- We expect the project to **be completed**. (passive voice used for *complete*; now *the project* is raised to object)
- The project **is expected** to **be completed**. (double passive)

Other verbs which can behave similarly to *expect* in such constructions include *order, tell, persuade*, etc., leading to such double passives as *The man was ordered to be shot* and *I was persuaded to be ordained.*

Similar constructions sometimes occur, however, when the first verb is raising-to-subject rather than raising-to-object – that is, when there is no object before the infinitive complement. For example, with *attempt*, the active voice construction is simply *We attempted to complete the project*. A double passive formed from that sentence would be:

- The project was attempted to be completed.

with both verbs changed simultaneously to the passive voice, even though the first verb takes no object – it is not possible to say **We attempted the project to be completed*, which is the sentence from which the double passive would appear to derive.

This latter double passive construction is criticized as questionable both grammatically and stylistically. Fowler calls it "clumsy and incorrect", suggesting that it springs from false analogy with the former (acceptable) type of double passive, though conceding its usefulness in some legal and quasi-legal language. Other verbs mentioned (besides *attempt*) with which the construction is found include ***begin, desire,*** *hope, propose, seek* and *threaten*. Similarly, *The American Heritage Book of English Usage* declares this construction unacceptable. It nonetheless occurs in practice in a variety of contexts.

## Additional passive constructions

Certain other constructions are sometimes classed as passives. The following types are mentioned by Pullum.

A *bare passive clause* is similar to a typical passive clause, but without the passive auxiliary verb (so it is a non-finite clause consisting of a subject together with a verb phrase based on a past participle with the passive construction). These can be used in such contexts as newspaper headlines:

- City hall damaged by hail

and as modifiers (adverbial phrases), i. e. nominative absolutes:

- **Our work done**, we made our way back home.
- **That said**, there are also other considerations.

Other constructions are mentioned in which a passive past participle clause is used, even though it is not introduced by the auxiliary *be* or *get* (or is introduced by *get* with a direct object):

- I had my car cleaned by a professional.
- Jane had her car stolen last week.
- You ought to get that lump looked at.
- This software comes pre-installed by the manufacturer.

In the *concealed passive*, the present participle or gerund form (*-ing* form) appears rather than the past participle. This can appear after *need*, and for some speakers after *want* (with similar meaning). For example:

- Your car needs washing. (meaning "needs to be washed"; some speakers might say *needs washed*)
- That rash needs looking at by a specialist.
- His hair wants cutting.

(An idiomatic expression with the same construction is... *doesn't bear thinking about*.) The verbs *need* and *want* also have similar uses with an object:

- I need/want my room painting.

Middle voice and passival

The term *middle voice* is sometimes used to refer to verbs used without a passive construction, but in a meaning where the grammatical subject is understood as undergoing the action. The meaning may be reflexive:

- Fred shaved, *i. e.* Fred shaved himself

but is not always:

- These cakes sell well, *i. e.* [we] sell these cakes [successfully]
- The clothes are soaking, *i. e.* [the water] is soaking the clothes

Such verbs may also be called *passival*.

Another construction sometimes referred to as *passival* involves a wider class of verbs, and was used in English until the nineteenth century. Sentences having this construction feature progressive aspect and resemble the active voice, but with meaning like the passive. Examples of this would be:

- The house is building (modern English: The house is being built)
- The meal is eating, (modern English: The meal is being eaten)

A rare example of the passival form being used in modern English is with the following phrase:

- The drums are beating, *i. e.* the drums are being beaten

This passival construction was displaced during the late 18th and early 19th century by the progressive passive (the formis *being built* as given above). The grammaticality of the progressive passive, called by some the "imperfect passive," was controversial among grammarians in the 19th century, but is accepted without question today. It has been suggested that the passive progressive appeared just to the east of Bristol and was popularized by the Romantic poets.

## COMMON GRAMMAR MISTAKES: ACTIVE VERSUS PASSIVE VOICE

### Active Voice

In the *active voice* the subject is doing an action– specifically, the action outlined by the verb. Since the subject is *active* in whatever the verb calls for, it's referred to as the active voice. This is found in most English sentences.

An example of the active voice would be: Stefanie loves dogs.

The subject of this sentence — in this case, *Stefanie*– is doing the action: the subject is, in essence, doing the loving. The word *dogs* in this instance, is the direct object, the receiver of this loving. Again, since the subject is active in doing, this sentence is in the *active voice.*

## Passive Voice

In the passive voice, these roles are reversed. The direct object moves to the subject's position and, in turn, the subject becomes the direct object. This role reversal is interesting because the focus of the sentence changes, allowing for the subject to receive the action, while the direct object does what the verb describes. So, instead of the active "Stefanie loves dogs", the sentence then becomes:

The dogs are loved by Stefanie.

In this instance, the subject, *the dogs,* aren't active in doing anything. They are just sitting there as the direct object, Stefanie, does all the action– in this case, all the loving. Lucky them.

The passive voice can also be phrased like this: "The dogs are being loved by Stefanie." This is also valid as it's still in the present tense and the subject is still *passive.*

## "So, is using passive voice wrong?"

Not necessarily. However, it can obfuscate your writing so it's best to use it sparingly. The active voice is direct and (ideally) to the point– this is clearly the best for academic writing and admission essays. It's encouraged to use the active voice because of its clarity and is a great way to make your writing tighter and more concise.

That being said, passive voice does well when writing reports, scientific studies, or anything else that requires objectivity over subjectivity. This is one of the major reasons why scientific studies and police reports are written largely in the passive voice– the writer has to be objective and not insert themselves into the work as a subject or, if the subject is unknown, hypothesize who or what that might be.

Passive voice can also be used creatively, particularly when writing fiction. The passive voice can denote a sense of mystery– "he was killed suddenly in the night," for instance– and can also create suspense. This is also more reason why it *shouldn't* be used in admissions or academic writing.

So, a few words of advice:

- The active voice means the subject is *active* in whatever the verb is doing. The subject is doing whatever the verb says it is.
- The passive is the opposite– it's not doing it but, instead, *receiving* it. The direct object is the one doing the work.
- Not every sentence in the passive voice has to have the verb *to be* in it. The verb phrase *I am*is a form of the verb *to be* which, as I'm sure you can figure out, is very much in the active voice.
- It's not necessarily incorrect to use the passive voice, but avoid it unless writing fiction, an objective report of some kind, or a scientific study.

# Chapter-2

# Adjectives

## ADJECTIVE

In linguistics, an **adjective** is a describing word, the mainsyntactic role of which is to qualify a noun or noun phrase, giving more information about the object signified. Adjectives are one of the English parts of speech, although historically they were classed together with the nouns. Certain words that were traditionally considered to be adjectives, including *the, this, my,* etc., are today usually classed separately, as determiners.

### Etymology

*Adjective* comes from Latin *(nômen) adjectîvum*"additional (noun)", a calque ofAncient Greek: ðßèåôïí (Dîïìá) *epítheton (ónoma)*"additional (noun)". In the grammatical tradition of Latin and Greek, because adjectives were inflected for gender, number, and case like nouns (a process called declension), they were considered a subtype of noun. The words that are today typically called nouns were then called*substantive nouns* (*nômen substantîvum*). The terms *noun substantive* and *noun adjective* were formerly used in English, until the word *noun* came to refer only to the former type, and the second type came to be known simply as adjectives.

### Types of use

A given occurrence of an adjective can generally be classified into one of three kinds of use:

1. Attributive adjectives are part of the noun phrase headed by the noun they modify; for example, happy is an attributive adjective in "happy people". In some languages, attributive adjectives precede their nouns; in others, they follow their nouns; and in yet others, it depends on the adjective, or on the exact relationship of the adjective to the noun. In English, attributive adjectives usually precede their nouns in simple phrases, but often follow their nouns when the adjective is modified or qualified by a phrase acting as an adverb. For example: "I saw three happy kids", and "I saw three kids happy enough to jump up and down with glee."
3. Predicative adjectives are linked via a copula or other linking mechanism to the noun or pronoun they modify; for example, happy is a predicate adjective in "they are happy" and in "that made me happy."
3. Nominal adjectives act almost as nouns. One way this can happen is if a noun is elided and an attributive adjective is left behind. In the sentence, "I read two books to them; he preferred the sad book, but she preferred the happy", *happy* is a nominal adjective, short for "happy one" or "happy book". Another way this can happen is in phrases like "out with the old, in with the new", where "the old" means, "that which is old" or "all that is old", and similarly with "the new". In such cases, the adjective functions either as a mass noun (as in the preceding example) or as a pluralcount noun, as in "The meek shall inherit the Earth", where "the meek" means "those who are meek" or "all who are meek".

## Distribution

Adjectives feature as a part of speech (word class) in most languages. In some languages, the words that serve thesemantic function of adjectives may be categorized together with some other class, such as nouns or verbs. For example, rather than an adjective meaning "big", a language might have a verb that means "to be big", and could then use anattributive verb construction analogous to "big-being house" to express what English expresses as "big house". Such an analysis is possible for the Chinese languages, for example.

Different languages do not always use adjectives in exactly the same situations. For example, where English uses *to be hungry* (*hungry* being an adjective), Dutch and French use *honger hebben* and *avoir faim* respectively (literally "to have hunger", the words for "hunger" being nouns). Similarly, where Hebrew uses the adjective æ÷å÷ *zaqûq* (roughly "in need of"), English uses the verb "to need".

In languages which have adjectives as a word class, they are usually an open class; that is, it is relatively common for new adjectives to be formed via such processes as derivation. However, Bantu languages are well known for having only a small closed class of adjectives, and new adjectives are not easily derived. Similarly, native Japanese adjectives (*i*-adjectives) are considered a closed class (as are native verbs), although nouns (an open class) may be used in thegenitive to convey some adjectival meanings, and there is also the separate open class of adjectival nouns (*na*-adjectives).

## Adjectives and adverbs

Many languages, including English, distinguish between adjectives, which qualify nouns and pronouns, and adverbs, which mainly modify verbs, adjectives, and other adverbs. Not all languages have exactly this distinction and many languages, including English, have words that can function as both. For example, in English *fast* is an adjective in "a **fast** car" (where it qualifies the noun *car*), but an adverb in "he drove fast" (where it modifies the verb *drove*).

In Dutch and German, adjectives and adverbs are usually identical in form and many grammarians do not make the distinction, but patterns of inflection can suggest a difference:

*Eine **kluge** neue Idee.*

A **clever** new idea.

*Eine **klug** ausgereifte Idee.*

A **cleverly** developed idea.

A German word like *klug* ("clever(ly)") takes endings when used as an attributive adjective, but not when used adverbially. (It also takes no endings when used as a predicative adjective:

*er ist klug*, "he is clever".) Whether these are distinct parts of speech or distinct usages of the same part of speech is a question of analysis. It is worth noting that while German linguistic terminology distinguishes *adverbiale* from *adjektivische Formen*, school German refers to both as*Eigenschaftswörter* ("property words").

## Determiners

Linguists today distinguish determiners from adjectives, considering them to be two separate parts of speech (or *lexical categories*), but formerly determiners were considered to be adjectives in some of their uses. In English dictionaries, which typically still do not treat determiners as their own part of speech, determiners are often recognizable by being listed both as adjectives and as pronouns. Determiners are words that are neither nouns nor pronouns, yet reference a thing already in context. Determiners generally do this by indicating definiteness (as in *a* vs. *the*), quantity (as in *one* vs. *some* vs. *many*), or another such property.

## Adjective phrases

An adjective acts as the head of an *adjective phrase* or *adjectival phrase* (AP). In the simplest case, an adjective phrase consists solely of the adjective; more complex adjective phrases may contain one or more adverbs modifying the adjective ("*very* strong"), or one or more complements (such as "worth *several dollars*", "full *of toys*", or "eager *to please*"). In English, attributive adjective phrases that include complements typically follow the noun that they qualify ("an evildoer*devoid of redeeming qualities*").

## Other modifiers of nouns

In many languages, including English, it is possible for nouns to modify other nouns. Unlike adjectives, nouns acting as modifiers (called *attributive nouns* or *noun adjuncts*) usually are not predicative; a beautiful park is beautiful, but a car park is not "car". The modifier often indicates origin ("*Virginia* reel"), purpose ("*work* clothes"), or semantic patient ("*man* eater");

however, it may generally indicate almost any semantic relationship. It is also common for adjectives to be derived from nouns, as in *boyish, birdlike, behavioral (behavioural), famous, manly, angelic,* and so on.

Many languages have special verbal forms called participles that can act as noun modifiers (alone or as the head of a phrase). Sometimes participles develop into pure adjectives. Examples of this in English include *relieved* (the past participle of the verb *relieve,* used as an adjective in sentences such as "I am so relieved to see you"), *spoken* (as in "the spoken word"), and *going* (the present participle of the verb *go,* used as an adjective in such phrases as "the going rate").

Other constructs that often modify nouns include prepositional phrases (as in "a rebel *without a cause*"), relative clauses(as in "the man *who wasn't there*"), and infinitive phrases (as in "a cake *to die for*"). Some nouns can also take complements such as content clauses (as in "the idea *that I would do that*"), but these are not commonly consideredmodifiers. For more information about possible modifiers and dependents of nouns, see Components of noun phrases.

## Adjective order

In many languages, attributive adjectives usually occur in a specific order. In general, the adjective order in English is:

1. Determiners — articles, adverbs, and other limiters.
2. Observation — postdeterminers and limiter adjectives (e. g., a real hero, a perfect idiot) and adjectives subject to subjective measure (e. g., beautiful, interesting), or objects with a value (e. g., best, cheapest, costly)
3. Size and shape — adjectives subject to objective measure (e. g., wealthy, large, round), and physical properties such as speed.
4. Age — adjectives denoting age (e. g., young, old, new, ancient, six-year-old).
5. Color — adjectives denoting color (e. g., red, black, pale).
6. Origin — denominal adjectives denoting source of noun (e. g., French, American, Canadian).

7. Material — denominal adjectives denoting what something is made of (e. g., woolen, metallic, wooden).
8. Qualifier — final limiter, often regarded as part of the noun (e. g., rocking chair, hunting cabin, passenger car, book cover).

This means that in English, adjectives pertaining to size precede adjectives pertaining to age ("little old", not "old little"), which in turn generally precede adjectives pertaining to color ("old white", not "white old"). So, we would say "One (quantity) nice (opinion) little (size) round (shape) old (age) white (color) brick (material) house."

This order may be more rigid in some languages than others; in some, like Spanish, it may only be a default (*unmarked*) word order, with other orders being permissible.

Due partially to borrowings from French, English has some adjectives that follow the noun as postmodifiers, called postpositive adjectives, as in *time immemorial* and *attorney general*. Adjectives may even change meaning depending on whether they precede or follow, as in *proper*: *They live in a proper town* (a real town, not a village) vs. *They live in the town proper* (in the town itself, not in the suburbs). All adjectives can follow nouns in certain constructions, such as *tell me something new*.

## Comparison of adjectives

In many languages, some adjectives are *comparable*. For example, a person may be "polite", but another person may be "more polite", and a third person may be the "most polite" of the three. The word "more" here modifies the adjective "polite" to indicate a comparison is being made, and "most" modifies the adjective to indicate an absolute comparison (a*superlative*).

Among languages that allow adjectives to be compared, different means are used to indicate the comparison. Many languages do not distinguish comparative from superlative forms.

In English, there are three different means to indicate comparison: most simple adjectives take the suffixes "-er" and "-est", as "big", "bigger", "biggest";

a very few adjectives are *irregular*:

"good", "better", "best",

"bad", "worse", "worst",

"old", "elder", "eldest" (in certain contexts only)

"far", "farther/further", "farthest/furthest"

"many", "more", "most" (usually regarded as an adverb or determiner)

"little", "less", "least";

all others are compared by means of the words "more" and "most". There is no simple rule to decide which means is correct for any given adjective, however. The general tendency is for simpler adjectives, and those from Anglo-Saxon to take the suffixes, while longer adjectives and those from French, Latin, Greek do not—but sometimes *sound* of the word is the deciding factor.

Many adjectives do not naturally lend themselves to comparison. For example, some English speakers would argue that it does not make sense to say that one thing is "more ultimate" than another, or that something is "most ultimate", since the word "ultimate" is already absolute in its semantics. Such adjectives are called *non-comparable* or *absolute*. Nevertheless, native speakers will frequently play with the raised forms of adjectives of this sort. Although "pregnant" is logically non-comparable (either one is pregnant or not), one may hear a sentence like "She looks more and more pregnant each day". Likewise "extinct" and "equal" appear to be non-comparable, but one might say that a language about which nothing is known is "more extinct" than a well-documented language with surviving literature but no speakers, while George Orwellwrote "All animals are equal, but some are more equal than others". These cases may be viewed as evidence that the base forms of these adjectives are not as absolute in their semantics as is usually thought.

Comparative and superlative forms are also occasionally used for other purposes than comparison. In English comparatives can be used to suggest that a statement is only tentative or tendential: one might say "John is more the shy-and-retiring type," where the comparative "more" is not really comparing him with other people or with other impressions of him, but rather, could be substituting for "on the whole". In Italian, superlatives are frequently used to put strong emphasis on an adjective: *Bellissimo* means "most beautiful", but is in fact more commonly heard in the sense "extremely beautiful".

## RESTRICTIVENESS

Attributive adjectives, and other noun modifiers, may be used either *restrictively* (helping to identify the noun's referent, hence "restricting" its reference) or *non-restrictively* (helping to describe an already-identified noun). For example:

"He was a lazy sort, who would avoid a **difficult task** and fill his working hours with easy ones."

"difficult" is restrictive - it tells us which tasks he avoids, distinguishing these from the easy ones: "Only those tasks that are difficult".

"She had the job of sorting out the mess left by her predecessor, and she performed this **difficult task** with great acumen." "difficult" is non-restrictive - we already know which task it was, but the adjective describes it more fully: "The aforementioned task, which (by the way) is difficult"

In some languages, such as Spanish, restrictiveness is consistently marked; for example, in Spanish *la tarea difícil* means "the difficult task" in the sense of "the task that is difficult" (restrictive), whereas *la difícil tarea* means "the difficult task" in the sense of "the task, which is difficult" (non-restrictive). In English, restrictiveness is not marked on adjectives, but is marked on relative clauses (the difference between "the man *who recognized me* was there" and "the man, *who recognized me*, was there" being one of restrictiveness).

### Agreement

In some languages, adjectives alter their form to reflect the gender, case and number of the noun that they describe. This is called agreement or concord. Usually it takes the form of inflections at the end of the word, as in Latin:

| | |
|---|---|
| *puella bon**a*** | (good girl, feminine) |
| *puell**am** bon**am*** | (good girl, feminine accusative/object case) |
| *puer bon**us*** | (good boy, masculine) |
| *pueri bon**i*** | (good boys, masculine plural) |

In the Celtic languages, however, initial consonant lenition marks the adjective with a feminine noun, as in Irish:

| | |
|---|---|
| *buachaill **maith*** | (good boy, masculine) |
| *girseach **mhaith*** | (good girl, feminine) |

Often a distinction is made here between attributive and predicative usage. Whereas English is an example of a language in which adjectives never agree and French of a language in which they always agree, in German they agree only when used attributively, and in Hungarian only when used predicatively.

| | |
|---|---|
| *The good (Ø) boys.* | *The boys are good (Ø).* |
| *Les bon**s** garçons.* | *Les garçons sont bon**s**.* |
| *Die brav**en** Jungen.* | *Die Jungen sind brav (Ø).* |
| *A jó (Ø) fiúk.* | *A fiúk jó**k**.* |

## Adjective

An **adjective** is a kind of word that modifies a noun. Nouns are words thatname a place, a person, a thing, or an idea. An adjective is a word that gives more information about the noun that goes with it.

As a rule, in English, the adjective comes before the noun it describes. It is also a part of speech.

## Exceptions

Sometimes an adjective is not followed by a noun:

- The sky is **blue**.
- The joke she told was so **funny**, I could not stop laughing all day.
- He went **crazy**.

- It's still an adjective, because we could have "the blue sky", "the funny joke", and "the crazy man". The adjective is still describing the noun though they are not side by side.
- There is a **tall** man.

An adjective is a word that gives instant information about a noun to make a clear picture of the noun in the mind of the reader and create a feeling of the writer.

## Comparative and Superlative

Sometimes there are different forms of the same adjective. If one joke makes a person laugh more than another joke, then that joke is **funnier**. This is called the comparative form of the adjective. The day that is colder than any other is the**coldest** day. This is the superlative form of "cold". Some adjectives need additional words when we want to compare them. For instance, one car may be **cheaper** than another, but the second car may be **more reliable**. (We use "more reliable", instead of "reliabler".) Reliable means worthy of trust.

The rule is:

For short adjectives ending in a consonant like "cold," "black," or "fast," one adds the suffix **er** to make a comparison of greater magnitude. Example: "The North Pole is colder than Florida." The greatest possible comparison is made by adding the suffix **est**. Example: "The North Pole is the coldest place on the Earth." For long adjectives like intelligent, conscientious, comprehensive, one uses the word **more** to make a comparison of greater magnitude. Example: "Children are more intelligent than adults." To make the greatest possible comparison one uses the word **most**. Example: "She is the most conscientious person I have ever known."

## Nouns as noun modifiers

In the English language, it is possible for a noun to modify (describe) another noun. Example: take the noun "angel" and the noun "face." Put them together and the result is "angel face." The first noun is acting like an adjective, because it is giving us information about the second noun.

## Adjectives and adverbs

Adjectives are words we use to describe the noun. Simple words like sparkling and fat are both adjectives commonly used in writing. One can make adverbs from some adjectives by adding the suffix **ly**. Example: take the adjective "beautiful," the adverb is beautifully. One can do it the other way around: take an adverb like "presumably," the adjective is "presumable" (assumable). "Presumable innocence" means the accused is assumed to be innocent until proven guilty (which is not always practiced everywhere, however).

The adjective "guilty" becomes the adverb "guiltily" and vice versa (the other way round)(the opposite), the adverb "guiltily" becomes the adjective "guilty." As a rule, "dogs chase cats" but not vice versa. Cats seldom chase dogs.

## Postpositive adjective

A **postpositive** or **postnominal adjective** is an attributive adjective that is placed after the noun or pronoun that it modifies. This contrasts with **prepositive adjectives**, which come before the noun or pronoun.

In some languages (such as French, Spanish, Italian and Romanian) the postpositive placement of adjectives is the normalsyntax, but in English it is less usual, largely confined to archaic and poetic uses (as in *They heard creatures **unseen***), certain traditional phrases (such as *heir **apparent***), and certain particular grammatical constructions (as in *those **anxious**to leave*).

Recognizing postpositive adjectives in English is important for determining the correct plural for a compound expression. For example, because *martial* is a postpositive adjective in the phrase *court-martial*, the plural is *courts-martial*, the ending being attached to the noun rather than the adjective.

## In languages where adjectives normally follow nouns

In certain languages, including French, Italian, Spanish, Romanian and Khmer, postpositive adjectives are the norm – that is to say, it is normal for an attributive adjective to follow, rather than precede, the noun it modifies. The following example is from French:

- *les chevaux* ***blancs,*** "the **white** horses", literally "the horses **white**"

In particular instances, however, such languages may also feature prepositive adjectives. In French, certain common adjectives normally precede the noun; these include *grand* ("big"), as in:

- *les* ***grands*** *chevaux,* "the **big** horses"

In many other languages, including English, German, Russian and Chinese, prepositive adjectives are the norm (attributive adjectives normally come before the nouns they modify), and adjectives appear postpositively only in special situations, if at all. The situations in which postpositive adjectives appear in English are described in the following sections.

## IN MODERN ENGLISH

### General uses

One common situation in which adjectives appear postpositively in English is when they qualify compound indefinite pronouns: *something, anyone, nobody, somewhere,* etc. Examples: *We need someone* ***strong****; Going anywhere* ***nice****?; Nothing* ***important*** *happened.*

Another situation is when the adjective itself has a modifier that comes after it; that is, when the noun or pronoun is in fact modified by an adjective phrase in which the head adjective is not final. Such phrases as *bigger than that, proud of themselves, anxious to leave,* if used attributively, would normally have to come after the noun, as in *we need a box* ***bigger****than that* (not **a bigger than that box,* although it is possible in this case to say *a bigger box than that*). Exceptions include certain established phrases such as *easy-to-use* and variations thereof, which can be used as if they were single adjectives before the noun. Phrases in which the adjective is followed only by *enough* also often appear before the noun. Conversely, some phrases in which the adjective is final, such as *this big* and *that ugly*, tend to follow the noun.

Certain adjectives are used fairly commonly in postpositive position. Present and past participles exhibit this behavior, as inall *those **entering** should..., one of the men **executed** was...*, but this may be considered to be a verbal rather than adjectival use (a kind of reduced relative clause). Similar behavior is displayed by many adjectives with the suffix *-able* or *-ible* (e. g. *the best room **available**, the only decision **possible**, the worst choice **imaginable***). Certain other adjectives with a sense similar to those in the foregoing categories are also found postpositively (*all the people **present**, the first paymentdue*).

Adjectives may undergo a change of meaning when used postpositively. Consider the following examples:

1. Every ***visible** star* is named after a famous astronomer.
2. Every *star **visible*** is named after a famous astronomer.

The postpositive in the second sentence is expected to refer to the stars that are visible here and now; that is, it expresses a stage-level predicate. The prepositive in the first sentence may also have that sense, but it may also have an individual-level meaning, referring to an inherent property of the object (the stars that are visible in general). Quite a significant difference in meaning is found with the adjective *responsible*:

1. I'm here to find the ***responsible** people.*
2. I'm here to find the *people **responsible**.*

Used prepositively, as in the first sentence, it generally means something like "trustworthy" or "reliable", but when used postpositively, as in the second sentence, it probably means "at fault" or "guilty" (of some misdeed known from the context). Another adjective with a special postpositive meaning is *proper*: in phrases like *the town **proper**, Sweden **proper***, it means something like "strictly defined".

## Set phrases

There are many set phrases in English which feature postpositive adjectives. They are often loans or loan translations from foreign languages that commonly use postpositives, especially French (many legal terms come from Law French). Some examples appear below:

- Legal and general terms: agent provocateur, battle royal, body corporate, body politic, corporation sole, court-martial, fee simple, fee tail, femme fatale, force majeure, God Almighty, heir apparent, heir presumptive, knight errant, language isolate, letters close, letters patent, life everlasting, the light fantastic, malice aforethought (also *malice prepense*), persona non grata, mens rea, pound sterling, proof positive, spaghetti bolognese, sum total, time immemorial, times past, treasure trove (in the legal sense)
- Names of posts, ranks, etc. : bishop emeritus, professor emeritus, etc.; attorney general, consul general, governor general, postmaster general, surgeon general, etc.; Astronomer Royal, Princess Royal, etc.; airman basic, minister plenipotentiary, minister-president, notary public, poet laureate, prime minister-designate, prince regent, sergeant major; queen consort, prince consort, etc.; queen regnant, prince regnant, etc.
- Various terms used in heraldry, including dexter and sinister (as in bend dexter, bend sinister), and several referring toattitude, as in eagle displayed, lion passant guardant, griffin rampant, phoenix rising, bird vigilant, etc.
- Names of organizations: Alcoholics Anonymous, Amnesty International, ARCHIVE Global, Child United, Church Universal and Triumphant, Generation Next, Japan Airlines Domestic, Jet-Blue, Ruritan National, Situationist International, Socialist International, Verizon Wireless, Virgin Mobile, Weather Underground, Workers United
- Hospital emergency codes: Code Amber, Code Black, Code Orange, Code Red
- Terms referring to food and drink: chicken supreme, etc.; whiskey sour, etc.
- Regnal numbers and other appellations, usually including the definite article before the adjective: Henry the Eighth, Elizabeth the Second, Alexander the Great, Ethelred the Unready, etc. Note also the generational titles *Junior*

and*Senior*, and a few special cases such as Nero Redivivus.

Certain other adjectives, or words of adjectival type, are typically placed after the noun, although their use is not limited to particular noun(s). Some of them may alternatively be regarded as adverbial modifiers, which would be expected to follow the noun. Examples of such uses include *buildings **ablaze**, two **abreast**, holidays **abroad**, fun and games **à gogo**, arms **akimbo**, food **aplenty**, athlete **extraordinaire**, tulips **galore**, devil **incarnate**, a hero **manqué**, the Cold War**redux**.*

## Archaic and poetic usage, titles of works

Phrases with postpositive adjectives are sometimes used with archaic effect, as in *things forgotten, words unspoken, dreams undreamt*. Phrases which reverse the normal word order are quite common in poetry, as with "fiddlers three" (from*Old King Cole*), "forest primeval" (from *Evangeline*).

Titles of books, films, etc. commonly feature nouns with postpositive adjectives. These are often present or past participles, but other types of adjectives sometimes occur. Examples: *Apocalypse Now Redux, Body Electric, Brideshead Revisited, Chronicle of a Death Foretold, A Dream Deferred, Hannibal Rising, Hercules Unchained, The Life Aquatic, A Love Supreme, The Matrix Reloaded, Monsters Unleashed, Orpheus Descending, Paradise Lost, Paradise Regained, Prometheus Unbound,* "The Road Not Taken", *Sonic Unleashed, Tarzan Triumphant, The World Unseen.*

## Other postpositive noun modifiers

Nouns may have other modifiers besides adjectives. Some kinds of modifiers tend to precede the noun, while others tend to come after. Determiners (including articles, possessives, demonstratives, etc.) come before the noun. Noun adjuncts(nouns qualifying another noun) also generally come before the nouns they modify: in a phrase like *book club*, the adjunct (modifier) *book* comes before the head (modified noun) *club*. However, prepositional phrases, adverbs of location, etc., as well as relative clauses, come after the nouns they modify: *the elephant **in the room**; all the people **here**; the woman **you spoke***

***to***. (These remarks apply to English syntax; other languages may use different word order. In Chinese, for example, virtually all modifiers come before the noun, whereas in the Khmer language they follow the noun.)

Sometimes a noun with a postpositive modifier comes to form a set phrase, similar in some ways to the set phrases with postpositive adjectives referred to above (in that, for example, the plural ending will normally attach to the noun, rather than at the end of the phrase). Some such phrases include:

- With a noun followed by a prepositional phrase: *mother-in-law* etc.; *editor-in-chief*, *right of way*, *president pro tempore*(where *pro tempore* is a Latin prepositional phrase), *fish filet deluxe* (where *de luxe* is a French prepositional phrase)
- With an infinitive verb or a verb phrase: *father-to-be*, *bride-to-be*, etc.; *Johnny-come-lately*
- With an adverbial particle from a phrasal verb: *passer-by*, *hanger-on*

In some phrases, a noun adjunct appears postpositively (rather than in the usual prepositive position). Examples includeKnights Hospitaller, Knights Templar, man Friday (or girl Friday, etc.), airman first class (also private first class, sergeant first class), as well as many names of foods and dishes, such as Bananas Foster, beef Wellington, broccoli raab, Cherries Jubilee, Chicken Tetrazzini, Crêpe Suzette, Eggs Benedict, Oysters Rockefeller, peach Melba, steak tartare, and duck a l'orange.

Identifying numbers (with or without the word *number*), and sometimes letters, appear after the noun in many contexts. Examples are *Catch-22*; warrant officer one, chief warrant officer two, etc.; Beethoven's Symphony No. 9; *Call of Duty Three*, *Rocky Four*, *Shrek the Third*, Generation Y. (For appellations such as "Henry the Fourth", often written "Henry IV", see above.)

Other common cases where modifiers follow a head noun include:

- Phrases like *the Brothers Grimm* and *the Sisters Rosensweig* (although in ordinary cases the phrasing "the Brown brothers" is more common)

- Names of military operations and equivalent, such as Operation Barbarossa, Operation Desert Storm, etc.
- Names of scientific projects and the like, such as Project Daedalus, Project Echo

## Plurals of expressions with postpositives

In the plural forms of expressions with postpositive adjectives or other postpositive modifiers, the pluralizing morpheme(most commonly the suffix *-s* or *-es*) is added after the noun, rather than after the entire phrase. For instance, the plural form of *town proper* is *towns proper*, that of *battle royal* is *battles royal*, that of *attorney general* is *attorneys general*, that of*bride-to-be* is *brides-to-be*, and that of *passer-by* is *passers-by*.

With some such expressions, there is a tendency (by way of regularization) to add the plural suffix to the end of the whole expression. This is usually regarded by prescriptive grammarians as an error. Examples are **queen consorts* (where*queens consort* is considered the correct form) and **court-martials* (where the accepted plural is *courts-martial*, although*court-martials* can be used as a third person present tense verb form).

This rule does not necessarily apply to phrases with postpositives that have been rigidly fixed into names and titles. (For example, an English speaker might say "Were there two separate Weather Undergrounds by the 1970s, or just one single organization?".) Other phrases remain as they are because they intrinsically use a plural construction (and have no singular form), such as *eggs Benedict, nachos supreme, Brothers Grimm, Workers United.*

## Proper adjective

In English orthography, the term **proper adjective** is sometimes applied to adjectives that take initial capital letters, and the term"**common adjective"** to those that do not. These terms are used informally only; they are not used by grammarians or linguists. For example, a person from Boston is a *Bostonian*. *Bostonian* is a proper adjective, and starts with a capital letter.

## Origin of the terms

The term "proper noun" denotes a noun that, grammatically speaking, identifies a specific unique entity; for example, *England* is a proper noun, because it is a name for a specific country, where as dog is not a proper noun — it is a "common noun" — because it is a term for any member of a group of animals.

In English orthography, most proper nouns are capitalized, while most common nouns are not. As a result, the term "proper noun" has come to mean, in lay usage, "a noun that is capitalized", and "common noun" to mean "a noun that is not capitalized". What's more, English adjectives that derive from proper nouns are usually capitalized. These two things, taken together, have led to the creation of the lay terms "proper adjective" and "common adjective" with meanings analogous to the lay meanings of "proper noun" and "common noun". Proper adjectives are just capitalized adjectives.

## Description of proper adjectives

In general, an adjective is capitalized if its meaning is "pertaining to *X*", where *X* is some specific person, place, language, or organized group. Most capitalized adjectives are derived from proper nouns; for example, the proper adjective *American* is derived from the proper noun *America*.

Sometimes, an adjective is capitalized because it designates an ethnic group with a shared culture, heritage, or ancestry. This usage asserts the existence of a unified group with common goals. For example, in Canadian government documents, *Native* and *Aboriginal* are capitalized.

An adjective can lose its capitalization when it takes on new meanings, such as *chauvinistic*. In addition, over time, an adjective can lose its capitalization by convention, generally when the word has overshadowed its original reference, such as *gargantuan, quixotic, titanic*, or *roman* in the term *roman numerals*.

### Proper adverbs

An adverb formed from a capitalized adjective is itself capitalized. For example:

- We have regularly received enquiries regarding the availability of IslamicFINANCE products, in particular Islamically compatible finance to purchase both residential and commercial properties.
- There are people who express themselves 'Frenchly,' while others have forms of life that are expressed 'Koreanly' or 'Icelandicly.'

### Other parts of speech

Verbs such as *Canadianize* are written with a capital letter, although not generally described as "proper verbs".

## COMMON ERRORS WITH ADJECTIVES

Incorrect: Every one knows this.

Correct: Everyone knows this.

### Explanation

**Everyone** should be written as one word.

Incorrect: He held the bag in the both hands.

Correct: He held the bag in both hands.

Correct: He held the bag in both his hands.

### Explanation

We do not use **the** before **both.**

Incorrect: Everybody should do some or other work.

Correct: Everybody should do some work or other.

Incorrect: Iron is more useful than any other metals.

Correct: Iron is more useful than any other metal.

Incorrect: Winston Churchill is greater than any other British politicians.

Correct: Winston Churchill is greater than any other British politician.

### Explanation

In these comparative sentences we should use a singular noun after **any other.**

Incorrect: He came a 3rd time.

Correct: He came a third time.

Incorrect: He is in class eighth.

Correct: He is in class eight.

Correct: He is in the eighth class.

Incorrect: He opened the book at six page.

Correct: He opened the book at page six.

Incorrect: This is a portrait of King George the sixth.

Correct: This is a portrait of King George VI.

### Explanation

The numbers of kings and queens should be written in Roman characters. Examples are: **Elizabeth II, Louis XIV**

Ordinal numbers (e. g. first, second, tenth etc.) up to twelfth should be written in words except in dates.

### Examples

**18th** October 2003 (NOT Eighteenth October 2003)

This is the **fifth** time you have asked the same question. (NOT This is the 5th time …)

Dates should be written as follows: July 7th or 7th July. (NOT 7th of July or seventh of July)

Cardinal numbers up to twelve should be written in words except when telling the time.

### Examples

He came at **10** am. (NOT He came at ten am.)

She has **seven** siblings. (NOT She has 7 siblings.)

Cardinal and ordinal numbers above twelve and twelfth may be written in either words or figures.

Incorrect: He is worst than you.

Correct: He is worse than you.

Incorrect: Mumbai is hot than Delhi.

Correct: Mumbai is hotter than Delhi.

## Explanation

Only an adjective or adverb in the comparative degree can be used before **than.**

Incorrect: A horse is usefuller than a car.

Correct: A horse is more useful than a car.

Adjectives and adverbs having more than one syllable form their comparative and superlative forms by the addition of **more** and **most.**

# Chapter-3

# Adverbs

An **adverb** is a word that modifies a verb, adjective, other adverb, determiner, noun phrase, clause, or sentence. Adverbs typically express manner, place, time, frequency, degree, level of certainty, etc., answering questions such as *how?*, *in what way?*, *when?*, *where?*, and *to what extent?*. This function is called the adverbialfunction, and may be realised by single words (adverbs) or by multi-word expressions (adverbial phrases and adverbial clauses).

Adverbs are traditionally regarded as one of the parts of speech. However, modern linguists note that it has come to be used as a kind of "catch-all" category, used to classify words with various different types of syntactic behavior, not necessarily having much in common except that they do not fit into any of the other available categories (noun, adjective, preposition, etc.)

## FUNCTIONS

The English word *adverb* derives (through French) from Latin *adverbium*, from *ad-* ("to"), *verbum* ("word", "verb"), and the nominal suffix *-ium*. The term implies that the principal function of adverbs is to act as modifiers of verbs or verb phrases. An adverb used in this way may provide information about the manner, place, time, frequency, certainty, or other circumstances of the activity denoted by the verb or verb phrase. Some examples:

- She sang **loudly** (*loudly* modifies the verb *sang*, indicating the manner of singing)
- We left it **here** (*here* modifies the verb phrase *left it*, indicating place)
- I worked **yesterday** (*yesterday* modifies the verb *worked*, indicating time)
- You **often** make mistakes (*often* modifies the verb phrase *make mistakes*, indicating frequency)
- He **undoubtedly** did it (*undoubtedly* modifies the verb phrase *did it*, indicating certainty)

Adverbs can also be used as modifiers of adjectives, and of other adverbs, often to indicate degree. Examples:

- You are **quite** right (the adverb *quite* modifies the adjective *right*)
- She sang **very** loudly (the adverb *very* modifies another adverb – *loudly*)

They can also modify noun phrases, prepositional phrases, or whole clauses orsentences, as in the following examples:

- I bought **only** the fruit (*only* modifies the noun phrase *the fruit*)
- She drove us **almost** to the station (*almost* modifies the prepositional phrase *to the station*)
- **Certainly** we need to act (*certainly* modifies the sentence as a whole)

Adverbs are thus seen to perform a wide range of modifying functions. The major exception is the function of modifier ofnouns, which is performed instead by adjectives (compare *she sang loudly* with *her loud singing disturbed me*; here the verb *sang* is modified by the adverb *loudly*, whereas the noun *singing* is modified by the adjective *loud*). However, as seen above, adverbs may modify noun *phrases*, and so the two functions may sometimes be superficially very similar:

- **Even** camels need to drink
- **Even** numbers are divisible by two

The word *even* in the first sentence is an adverb, since it is an "external" modifier, modifying *camels* as a noun phrase (compare *even these camels...)*, whereas the word *even* in the second sentence is an adjective, since it is an "internal" modifier, modifying *numbers* as a noun (compare *these even numbers...).* It is nonetheless possible for certain adverbs to modify a noun; in English the adverb follows the noun in such cases, as in:

- The people **here** are friendly
- The show features dances **galore**
- There is a shortage **internationally** of protein for animal feeds

Adverbs can sometimes be used as predicative expressions; in English this applies especially to adverbs of location:

- Your seat is **there**.

When the function of an adverb is performed by an expression consisting of more than one word, it is called an adverbial phrase or adverbial clause, or simply an adverbial.

## Formation and comparison

In English, adverbs of manner (answering the question *how?*) are often formed by adding *-ly* to adjectives. Other languages often have similar methods for deriving adverbs from adjectives (French, for example, uses the suffix *-ment*), or else use the same form for both adjectives and adverbs. Many other adverbs, however, are not related to adjectives in this way; they may be derived from other words or phrases, or may be single morphemes. Examples of such adverbs in English include*here, there, together, yesterday, aboard, very, almost*, etc.

Where the meaning permits, adverbs may undergo comparison, taking comparative and superlative forms. In English this is usually done by adding *more* and *most* before the adverb (*more slowly, most slowly*), although there are a few adverbs that take inflected forms, such as *well*, for which *better* and *best* are used.

For more information about the formation and use of adverbs in English, see English grammar: Adverbs. For other languages, see In specific languages below, and the articles on individual languages and their grammars.

## Adverbs as a "catch-all" category

Adverbs are considered a part of speech in traditional English grammar, and are still included as a part of speech in grammar taught in schools and used in dictionaries. However, modern grammarians recognize that words traditionally grouped together as adverbs serve a number of different functions. Some describe adverbs a "catch-all" category that includes all words that do not belong to one of the other parts of speech.

A logical approach to dividing words into classes relies on recognizing which words can be used in a certain context. For example, the only type of word that can be inserted in the following template to form a grammatical sentence is a noun:

The _____ is red. (For example, "The hat is red".)

When this approach is taken, it is seen that adverbs fall into a number of different categories. For example, some adverbs can be used to modify an entire sentence, whereas others cannot. Even when a sentential adverb has other functions, the meaning is often not the same. For example, in the sentences *She gave birth naturally* and *Naturally, she gave birth*, the word *naturally* has different meanings: as a sentential adverb it means something like "of course", while as a verb-modifying adverb it means "in a natural manner".

Words like *very* afford another example. We can say *Perry is very fast*, but not *Perry very won the race*. These words can modify adjectives but not verbs. On the other hand, there are words like *here* and *there* that cannot modify adjectives. We can say *The sock looks good there* but not *It is a there beautiful sock*. The fact that many adverbs can be used in more than one of these functions can confuse the issue, and it may seem like splitting hairs to say that a single adverb is really two or more words that serve different functions. However, this distinction can be useful, especially when considering adverbs like *naturally* that have different meanings in their different functions. Rodney Huddleston distinguishes between a*word* and a *lexicogram-matical-word*.

Grammarians find difficulty categorizing negating words, such as the English *not*. Although traditionally listed as an adverb, this word does not behave grammatically like any other, and it probably belongs in a class on its own.

## Prepositional adverb

A **prepositional adverb** is a word - mainly a particle - which is very similar in its form to a preposition but functions as anadverb. Prepositional adverbs occur, for example, in English, German and Dutch. Unlike real prepositions, they occur mainly at the end of a phrase and not before nouns. They also modify the verb, which a preposition does not.

An example of a prepositional adverb in English is *inside* in *He came inside.*

## Phrasal verb

A verb combined with a prepositional adverb is called a phrasal verb only if the verb's meaning is changed by the prepositional adverb. In English, there are lots of examples of this. For example, *let* can have many possible meanings depending on which prepositional adverb it is combined with (*let down, let in, let off, let to* etc.)

## Prepositional adverbs in other languages

Although prepositional adverbs are largely associated with Germanic languages, those of other classes occasionally have corresponding features. For instance, Slavic languages such as Czech may prefix prepositions to verbs of motion (*jít* to go '! *dojít* to come towards, *odejít* to go away from). In Hungarian, the suffixes added to nouns to perform the same functions as prepositions in Indo-European languages may also be prefixed to verbs, much as in German (*városba* to the city, *bemenni* to go towards).

## Pronominal adverb

A **pronominal adverb** is a type of adverb occurring in a number of Germanic languages, formed in replacement of apreposition and a pronoun by turning the latter into a locative adverb and the former into a prepositional adverb and joining them in reverse order.

For example:

- For that '! therefor
- In that '! therein
- By this '! hereby
- To this '! hereto
- In which '! wherein

Usage in English

In English, pronominal adverbs are most commonly encountered in literary registers or in legal usage. They are used frequently by lawyers and drafters of legal documents primarily as a way of avoiding the repetition of names of things in the document (or sometimes as a self-reference to the document itself). For this reason, pronominal adverbs are often seen as a type of legal jargon.

## Usage in Dutch

In Dutch, pronominal adverbs are very common and are almost mandatory in many situations; neglecting to use them often makes a phrase sound unnatural to native speakers. Dutch maintains a three-way distinction of reference in its demonstrative pronouns, with pronouns for things close by and far away, and a third pronoun that is unspecific for distance. This distinction is faithfully reflected in the use of pronominal adverbs, and other pronouns also often have a corresponding adverbial form.

## ADVER Definition

Adverbs are words that modify

- a **verb** (He drove slowly. — How did he drive?)
- an **adjective** (He drove a very fast car. — How fast was his car?)
- another adverb (She moved quite slowly down the aisle. — How slowly did she move?)

As we will see, adverbs often tell when, where, why, or under what conditions something happens or happened. Adverbs frequently end in *-ly*; however, many words and phrases not ending in *-ly* serve an adverbial function and an *-ly* ending is not a guarantee that a word is an adverb. The words *lovely, lonely, motherly, friendly, neighborly*, for instance, are adjectives:

- That lovely woman lives in a friendly neighborhood.

If a group of words containing a subject and verb acts as an adverb (modifying the verb of a sentence), it is called an **Adverb Clause:**

- When this class is over, we're going to the movies.

When a group of words not containing a subject and verb acts as an adverb, it is called an **adverbial phrase**. **Prepositional phrases**frequently have adverbial functions (telling place and time, modifying the verb):

- He went to the movies.
- She works on holidays.
- They**LIVED IN CANADA** during the war.

And **Infinitive phrases** can act as adverbs (usually telling why):

- She hurried to the mainland to see her brother.
- The senator ran to catch the bus.

But there are other kinds of adverbial phrases:

- He calls his mother as often as possible.

Adverbs can modify **adjectives**, but an adjective cannot modify an adverb. Thus we would say that "the students showed a really wonderful attitude" and that "the students showed a wonderfully casual attitude" and that "my professor is really tall, but not"He ran real fast."

Like adjectives, adverbs can have comparative and superlative forms to show degree.

- Walk faster if you want to keep up with me.
- The student who reads fastest will finish first.

We often use *more* and *most, less* and *least* to show degree with adverbs:

- With sneakers on, she could move more quickly among the patients.

- The flowers were the most beautifully arranged creations I've ever seen.
- She worked less confidently after her accident.
- That was the least skillfully done performance I've seen in years.

The as — as construction can be used to create adverbs that express sameness or equality: "He can't run as fast as his sister."

A handful of adverbs have two forms, one that ends in *-ly* and one that doesn't. In certain cases, the two forms have different meanings:

- He arrived late.
- Lately, he couldn't seem to be on time for anything.

In most cases, however, the form without the *-ly* ending should be reserved for casual situations:

- She certainly drives slow in that old Buick of hers.
- He did wrong by her.
- He spoke sharp, quick, and to the point.

Adverbs often function as **intensifiers**, conveying a greater or lesser emphasis to something. Intensifiers are said to have three different functions: they can emphasize, amplify, or downtone. Here are some examples:

- Emphasizers:
  - I really don't believe him.
  - He literally wrecked his mother's car.
  - She simply ignored me.
  - They're going to be late, for sure.
- Amplifiers:
  - The teacher completely rejected her proposal.
  - I absolutely refuse to attend any more faculty meetings.
  - They heartily endorsed the new restaurant.
  - I so wanted to go with them.
  - We know this city well.
- Downtoners:
  - I kind of like this college.
  - Joe sort of felt betrayed by his sister.

- o His mother mildly disapproved his actions.
- o We can improve on this to some extent.
- o The boss almost quit after that.
- o The school was all but ruined by the storm.

Adverbs (as well as adjectives) in their various degrees can be accompanied by premodifiers.

- She runs very fast.
- We're going to run out of material all the faster

This issue is addressed in the section on **degrees in adjectives**.

For this section on intensifiers, we are indebted to *A Grammar of Contemporary English* by Randolph Quirk, Sidney Greenbaum, Geoffrey Leech, and Jan Svartvik. Longman Group: London. 1978. pages 438 to 457. Examples our own.

## USING ADVERBS IN A NUMBERED LIST

Within the normal flow of text, it's nearly always a bad idea to number items beyond three or four, at the most. Anything beyond that, you're better off with a **vertical list** that uses numbers (1, 2, 3, etc.). Also, in such a list, don't use adverbs (with an *-ly* ending); use instead the uninflected ordinal number (first, second, third, fourth, fifth, etc.). First (not firstly), it's unclear what the adverb is modifying. Second (not secondly), it's unnecessary. Third (not thirdly), after you get beyond "secondly," it starts to sound silly. Adverbs that number in this manner are treated as *disjuncts*

### Adverbs We Can Do Without

Review the section on **Being Concise** for some advice on adverbs that we can eliminate to the benefit of our prose: **intensifiers** such as *very, extremely,* and *really* that don't intensify anything and **expletive constructions** ("There are several books that address this issue.")

### Kinds of Adverbs

**Adverbs of Manner**

She moved slowly and spoke quietly.

**Adverbs of Place**

She has lived on the island all her life.

She still lives there now.

**Adverbs of Frequency**

She takes the boat to the mainland every day.

She often goes by herself.

**Adverbs of Time**

She tries to get back before dark.

It's starting to get dark now.

She finished her tea first.

She left early.

## Adverbs of Purpose

She drives her boat slowly to avoid hitting the rocks.

She shops in several stores to get the best buys.

## Positions of Adverbs

One of the hallmarks of adverbs is their ability to move around in a sentence. Adverbs of manner are particularly flexible in this regard.

- Solemnly the minister addressed her congregation.
- The minister solemnly addressed her congregation.
- The minister addressed her congregation solemnly.

The following adverbs of frequency appear in various points in these sentences:

- Before the main verb: I never get up before nine o'clock.
- Between the auxiliary verb and the main verb: I have rarely written to my brother without a good reason.
- Before the verb *used to:* I always used to see him at his summer home.

Indefinite adverbs of time can appear either before the verb or between the auxiliary and the main verb:

- He finally showed up for batting practice.

- She has recently retired.
  Order of Adverbs
- There is a basic order in which adverbs will appear when there is more than one. It is similar to **The Royal Order of Adjectives**, but it is even more flexible.

## MORE NOTES ON ADVERB ORDER

As a general principle, shorter adverbial phrases precede longer adverbial phrases, regardless of content. In the following sentence, an adverb of time precedes an adverb of frequency because it is shorter (and simpler):

- Dad takes a brisk walk before breakfast every day of his life.

A second principle: among similar adverbial phrases of kind (manner, place, frequency, etc.), the more specific adverbial phrase comes first:

- My grandmother was born in a sod house on the plains of northern Nebraska.
- She promised to meet him for lunch next Tuesday.

Bringing an adverbial modifier to the beginning of the sentence can place special emphasis on that modifier. This is particularly useful with adverbs of manner:

- Slowly, ever so carefully, Jesse filled the coffee cup up to the brim, even above the brim.
- Occasionally, but only occasionally, one of these lemons will get by the inspectors.

### Inappropriate Adverb Order

Review the section on **Misplaced Modifiers** for some additional ideas on placement. Modifiers can sometimes attach themselves to and thus modify words that they ought not to modify.

- They reported that Giuseppe Balle, a European rock star, had died on the six o'clock news.

Clearly, it would be better to move the underlined modifier to a position immediately after "they reported" or even to the beginning of the sentence — so the poor man doesn't die on television.

Misplacement can also occur with very simple modifiers, such as *only* and *barely*:

- She only grew to be four feet tall.

  It would be better if "She grew to be only four feet tall."

## Adjuncts, Disjuncts, and Conjuncts

Regardless of its position, an adverb is often neatly integrated into the flow of a sentence. When this is true, as it almost always is, the adverb is called an adjunct. (Notice the underlined adjuncts or adjunctive adverbs in the first two sentences of this paragraph.) When the adverb does not fit into the flow of the clause, it is called a disjunct or a conjunct and is often set off by a comma or set of commas. A disjunct frequently acts as a kind of evaluation of the rest of the sentence. Although it usually modifies the verb, we could say that it modifies the entire clause, too. Notice how "too" is a disjunct in the sentence immediately before this one; that same word can also serve as an adjunct adverbial modifier: It's too hot to play outside. Here are two more disjunctive adverbs:

- Frankly, Martha, I don't give a hoot.
- Fortunately, no one was hurt.

Conjuncts, on the other hand, serve a connector function within the flow of the text, signaling a transition between ideas.

- If they start smoking those awful cigars, then I'm not staying.
- We've told the landlord about this ceiling again and again, and yet he's done nothing to fix it.

At the extreme edge of this category, we have the purely conjunctive device known as the conjunctive adverb (often called the adverbial conjunction):

- Jose has spent years preparing for this event; nevertheless, he's the most nervous person here.
- I love this school; however, I don't think I can afford the tuition.

Authority for this section: *A University Grammar of English* by Randolph Quirk and Sidney Greenbaum. Longman Group: Essex, England. 1993. 126. Used with permission. Examples our own.

## Some Special Cases

The adverbs *enough* and *not enough* usually take a postmodifier position:

- Is that music loud enough?
- These shoes are not big enough.
- In a roomful of elderly people, you must remember to speak loudly enough.

(Notice, though, that when *enough* functions as an adjective, it can come before the noun:

- Did she give us enough time?

The adverb *enough* is often followed by an infinitive:

- She didn't run fast enough to win.

The adverb *too* comes before adjectives and other adverbs:

- She ran too fast.
- She works too quickly.

If *too* comes after the adverb it is probably a disjunct (meaning *also*) and is usually set off with a comma:

- Yasmin works hard. She works quickly, too.

The adverb *too* is often followed by an infinitive:

- She runs too slowly to enter this race.

Another common construction with the adverb *too* is *too* followed by a prepositional phrase — *for* + the object of the preposition — followed by an infinitive:

- This milk is too hot for a baby to drink.

## Relative Adverbs

Adjectival clauses are sometimes introduced by what are called the **relative adverbs**: *where, when,* and *why*. Although the entire clause is adjectival and will modify a noun, the relative word itself fulfills an adverbial function (modifying a verb within its own clause).

The relative adverb *where* will begin a clause that modifies a noun of place:

My entire family now worships in the church where my great grandfather used to be minister.

The relative pronoun "where" modifies the verb "used to be" (which makes it adverbial), but the entire clause ("where my great grandfather used to be minister") modifies the word "church."

A *when* clause will modify nouns of time:

My favorite month is always February, when we celebrate Valentine's Day and Presidents' Day.

And a *why* clause will modify the noun *reason:*

Do you know the reason why Isabel isn't in class today?

We sometimes leave out the relative adverb in such clauses, and many writers prefer "that" to "why" in a clause referring to "reason":

- Do you know the reason ~~why~~ Isabel isn't in class today?
- I always look forward to the day ~~when~~ we begin our summer vacation.
- I know the reason that men like motorcycles.

Authority for this section: *Understanding English Grammar* by Martha Kolln. 4rth Edition. MacMillan Publishing Company: New York. 1994.

## Viewpoint, Focus, and Negative Adverbs

A **viewpoint adverb** generally comes after a noun and is related to an adjective that precedes that noun:

- A successful athletic team is often a good team scholastically.
- **INVESTING**all our money in snowmobiles was probably not a sound idea financially.

You will sometimes hear a phrase like "scholastically speaking" or "financially speaking" in these circumstances, but the word "speaking" is seldom necessary.

A **focus adverb** indicates that what is being communicated is limited to the part that is focused; a focus adverb will tend either to limit the sense of the sentence ("He got an A just for attending the class.") or to act as an additive ("He got an A in addition to being published."

Although negative constructions like the words "not" and "never" are usually found embedded within a verb string — "He has never been much help to his mother." — they are technically not part of the verb; they are, indeed, adverbs. However, a so-called **negative adverb** creates a negative meaning in a sentence *without* the use of the usual no/not/ neither/nor/never constructions:

- He seldom visits.
- She hardly eats anything since the accident.
- After her long and tedious lectures, rarely was anyone awake.

## Errors in the use of adverbs

Different kinds of **adverbs** go in different positions in a sentence. The usage is sometimes very different, too. ESL students often find it difficult to use adverbs correctly. Here are some common mistakes in the use of adverbs.

Incorrect: He plays tennis good.

Correct: He plays tennis well.

**Good** is an adjective. The adverb for this meaning is **well**.

Incorrect: I am very much sorry.

Correct: I am very sorry.

**Very** is used without **much** before adjectives and adverbs in the positive degree.

Incorrect: I am much tired.

Correct: I am very tired.

**Much** does not mean the same as **very.**

Incorrect: She is so poor to pay the dues.

Correct: She is too poor to pay the dues.

Incorrect: It is very hot to go out.

Correct: It is too hot to go out.

Note the structure **too...to.**

Incorrect: She carefully drove.

Correct: She drove carefully.

Incorrect: She angrily spoke.

Correct: She spoke angrily.

Adverbs of manner usually go in the end-position.

Incorrect: The room is enough spacious for us.

Correct: The room is spacious enough for us.

The adverb **enough** goes after the adjective or adverb it modifies.

Incorrect: I know to swim.

Correct: I know how to swim.

**Know** cannot be directly followed by an infinitive. Instead we use the structure **know how to**.

Incorrect: He is not clever to solve the problem.

Correct: He is not clever enough to solve the problem.

Incorrect: He is now too strong to walk.

Correct: He is now strong enough to walk.

Chapter-4

# Articles

## ARTICLE (GRAMMAR)

An **article** (abbreviated ART) is a word (or prefix or suffix) that is used with a noun to indicate the type of reference being made by the noun. Articles specify grammatical definiteness of the noun, in some languages extending to volume or numerical scope. The articles in the English language are *the* and *a/an*, and (in certain contexts) *some*. 'An' and 'a' are modern forms of the Old English 'an', which in Anglian dialects was the number 'one' (compare 'on', in Saxon dialects) and survived into Modern Scots as the number 'ane'. Both 'on' (respelled 'one' by the Normans) and 'an' survived into Modern English, with 'one' used as the number and 'an' ('a', before nouns that begin with a consonant sound) as an indefinite article.

Traditionally in English, an article is usually considered to be a type of adjective. In some languages, articles are a special part of speech, which cannot easily be combined with other parts of speech. It is also possible for articles to be part of another part of speech category such as a determiner, an English part of speech category that combines articles and demonstratives (such as 'this' and 'that').

In languages that employ articles, every common noun, with some exceptions, is expressed with a certain definiteness(e. g., definite or indefinite), just as many languages express every noun with a certain grammatical number (e. g., singular or plural). Every noun *must* be accompanied by the article, if any, corresponding to its definiteness, and the lack of an article (considered a *zero article*) itself specifies a certain definiteness. This is in contrast to other adjectives and determiners, which are typically optional. This obligatory nature of articles makes them among the most common words in many languages—in English, for example, the most frequent word is *the*.

Articles are usually characterized as either *definite* or *indefinite*. A few languages with well-developed systems of articles may distinguish additional subtypes. Within each type, languages may have various forms of each article, according to grammatical attributes such as gender, number, or case, or according to adjacent sounds.

## Definite article

A definite article indicates that its noun is a particular one (or ones) identifiable to the listener. It may be something that the speaker has already mentioned, or it may be something uniquely specified. The definite article in English, for both singular and plural nouns, is *the*.

***The children*** *know* ***the fastest way*** *home.*

The sentence above refers to specific children and a specific way home; it contrasts with the much more general observation that:

***Children*** *know* ***the fastest way*** *home.*

The latter sentence refers to children in general and their specific ways home. Likewise,

*Give me* ***the book.***

refers to a specific book whose identity is known or obvious to the listener; as such it has a markedly different meaning from

*Give me* ***a book.***

which does not specify what book is to be given.

The definite article can also be used in English to indicate a specific class among other classes:

*The cabbage white butterfly lays its eggs on members of the Brassica genus.*

However, recent developments show that definite articles are morphological elements linked to certain noun types due tolexicalization. Under this point of view, definiteness does not play a role in the selection of a definite article more than the lexical entry attached to the article.

The definite article is sometimes also used with proper names, which are already specified by definition (there *is* just one of them). For example: *the Amazon, the Hebrides*. In these cases, the definite article may be considered superfluous. Its presence can be accounted for by the assumption that they are shorthand for a longer phrase in which the name is a specifier, i. e. *the Amazon River, the Hebrides Islands*. Where the nouns in such longer phrases cannot be omitted, the definite article is universally kept: *the United States, the People's Republic of China*. This distinction can sometimes become a political matter: the former usage *the Ukraine* stressed the word's Russian meaning of "borderlands"; asUkraine became a fully independent state following the collapse of the Soviet Union, it requested formal mentions of its name omit the article. Similar shifts in usage have occurred in the names of Sudan and both Congo (Brazzaville) and(Kinshasa); a move in the other direction occurred with The Gambia.

Some languages also use definite articles with personal names. For example, such use is standard in Portuguese: *a Maria*, literally: "the Maria". It also occurs colloquially in Spanish, German and other languages, and is sometimes heard in Italian. In Hungary it is considered to be a Germanism.

## Indefinite article

An *indefinite* article indicates that its noun is not a particular one (or ones) identifiable to the listener. It may be something that the speaker is mentioning for the first time, or its precise identity may be irrelevant or hypothetical, or the speaker may be making a general statement about any such thing. English uses *a/an*, from the Old English forms of the number 'one', as its primary indefinite article. The form *an* is used before words that begin with a vowel sound (even if spelled with an initial consonant, as in *an hour*), and *a* before words that begin with a consonant sound (even if spelled with a vowel, as in *a European*).

*She had **a** house so large that **an** elephant would get lost without **a** map.*

Before some words beginning with a pronounced (not silent) *h* in an unstressed first syllable, such as *hallucination, hilarious, historic(al), horrendous,* and *horrific,* some (especially older) British writers prefer to use *an* over *a* (*an historical event,* etc.). *An* is also preferred before *HOTEL* by some writers of British English (probably reflecting the relatively recent adoption of the word from French, where the *h* is not pronounced). The use of "an" before words beginning with an unstressed "h" is more common generally in British English than American. American writers normally use *a* in all these cases, although there are occasional uses of *an historic(al)* in American English. According to the New Oxford Dictionary of English, such use is increasingly rare in British English too. Unlike British English, American English typically uses *an*before *herb,* since the *h* in this word is silent for most Americans. The correct usage in respect of the term "hereditary peer" was the subject of an amendment debated in the UK Parliament.

The word *some* is used as a functional plural of *a/an.*"An apple" never means more than one apple. "Give me *some* apples" indicates more than one is desired but without specifying a quantity. This finds comparison in Spanish, where the singular indefinite article 'un/una' ("one") is completely indistinguishable from the unit number, except where it has a plural form ('unos/unas'): *Dame una manzana" ("Give me an apple")* > "Dame *unas* manzanas" ("Give me some apples"). However, *some* also serves as a quantifier rather than as a plural article, as in "There are *some* apples there, but not many."

*Some* also serves as a singular indefinite article, as in "There is *some* person on the porch". This usage differs from the usage of *a(n)* in that *some* indicates that the identity of the noun is unknown to both the listener and the speaker, while *a(n)*indicates that the identity is unknown to the listener without specifying whether or not it is known to the speaker. Thus *There is some person on the porch* indicates indefiniteness to both the listener and the speaker, while *There is a person on the porch* indicates indefiniteness to the listener but gives no information as to whether the speaker knows the person's identity.

## Partitive article

A **partitive** article is a type of indefinite article used with a mass noun such as *water,* to indicate a non-specific quantity of it. Partitive articles are used in French and Italian in addition to definite and indefinite articles. The nearest equivalent in English is *some,* although this is considered a determiner and not an article.

French: *Veux tu **du** café ?*

*Do you want (**some**) coffee?* (or, dialectally but more accurately, *Do you want **some of this** coffee?*)

Haida has a partitive article (suffixed *-gyaa*) referring to "part of something or... to one or more objects of a given group or category,"e. g., *tluugyaa uu hal tlaahlaang* 'he is making a boat (a member of the category of boats). '

## Negative article

A **negative** article specifies *none* of its noun, and can thus be regarded as neither definite nor indefinite. On the other hand, some consider such a word to be a simple determiner rather than an article. In English, this function is fulfilled by *no,* which can appear before a singular or plural noun:***No** man has been on this island. **No** dogs are allowed here.*

***No** one is in London.*

## Zero article

The **zero article** is the absence of an article. In languages having a definite article, the lack of an article specifically indicates that the noun is indefinite. Linguists interested in X-bar theory causally link zero articles to nouns lacking a determiner. In English, the zero article rather than the indefinite is used with plurals and mass nouns, although the word "some" can be used as an indefinite plural article.

*Visitors end up walking in mud.*

## Variation among languages

Articles are found in many Indo-European, Semitic, and Polynesianlanguages but formally are absent from some large languages of the world, such as Indonesian, Japanese, Hindi and Russian.

Linguists believe the common ancestor of the Indo-European languages, Proto-Indo-European, did not have articles. Most of the languages in this family do not have definite or indefinite articles; there is no article in Latin, Sanskrit, nor in some modern Indo-European languages, such as the families of Slavic languages (not including Bulgarian, Macedonian and Torlakian, which are rather distinctive among the Slavic languages in terms of grammar) andBaltic languages. Although Classical Greek has a definite article (which has survived into Modern Greek and which bears strong resemblance to the German definite article), the earlier Homeric Greek used this article largely as a pronoun or demonstrative. Articles developed independently in several language families.

Not all languages have both definite and indefinite articles, and some languages have different types of definite and indefinite articles to distinguish finer shades of meaning; for example, French and Italian have a partitive article used for indefinite mass nouns, whereas Colognian has two distinct sets of definite articles indicating focus and uniqueness, and Macedonian uses definite articles in a demonstrative sense, with a tripartite distinction (proximal, medial, distal) based on distance from the speaker or interlocutor. The words *this* and *that* (and their plurals, *these* and*those*) can be understood in English as, ultimately, forms of the definite article *the* (whose declension in Old English included*thaes*, an ancestral form of this/that and these/those).

In many languages, the form of the article may vary according to the gender, number, or case of its noun. In some languages the article may be the only indication of the case. Many languages do not use articles at all, and may use other ways of indicating old versus new information, such as topic–comment constructions.

## Evolution

Articles have developed independently in many different language families across the globe. Generally, articles develop over time usually by specialization of certain adjectives.

Joseph Greenberg in Universals of Human Language describes "the cycle of the definite article": Definite articles (Stage I) evolve from demonstratives, and in turn can become generic articles (Stage II) that may be used in both definite and indefinite contexts, and later merely noun markers (Stage III) that are part of nouns other than proper names and more recent borrowings. Eventually articles may evolve anew from demonstratives.

## Definite articles

Definite articles typically arise from demonstratives meaning *that*. For example, the definite articles in the Romance languages—e. g., *el, il, le, la*—derive from the Latin demonstratives *ille* (masculine) and *illa* (feminine).

The English definite article *the,* written *þe* in Middle English, derives from an Old English demonstrative, which, according to gender, was written *se* (masculine), *seo* (feminine) (*þe* and *þeo* in the Northumbrian dialect), or *þæt* (neuter). The neuter form *þæt* also gave rise to the modern demonstrative *that*. The *ye* occasionally seen in pseudo-archaic usage such as "Ye Olde Englishe Tea Shoppe" is actually a form of *þe,* where the letter thorn (*þ*) came to be written as a *y*.

Multiple demonstratives can give rise to multiple definite articles. Macedonian, for example, in which the articles are suffixed, has *ñòîëîò* (*stolot*), the chair; *ñòîëîâ* (*stolov*), this chair; and *ñòîëîí* (*stolon*), that chair. These derive from the Common Slavic demonstratives **tú*"this, that", **ovú*"this here" and **onú*"that over there, yonder" respectively. Colognian prepositions articles such as in *dat Auto*, or *et Auto*, the car; the first being specifically selected, focussed, newly introduced, while the latter is not selected, unfocussed, already known, general, or generic. Standard Basque distinguishes between proximal and distal definite articles in the plural (dialectally, a proximal singular and an additional medial grade may also be present). The Basque distal form (with infix *-a-*, etymologically a suffixed and phonetically reduced form of the distal demonstrative *har-/hai-*) functions as the default definite article, whereas the proximal form (with infix *-o-*, derived from the proximal demonstrative *hau-/hon-*) is marked and indicates some kind of (spatial or otherwise) close relationship between the speaker and the referent (e. g., it may imply that the speaker is included in the referent): *etxeak* ("the houses") vs. *etxeok* ("these houses [of ours]"), *euskaldunak* ("the Basque speakers") vs. *euskaldunok* ("we, the Basque speakers").

## Indefinite articles

Indefinite articles typically arise from adjectives meaning *one*. For example, the indefinite articles in the Romance languages—e. g., *un, una, une*—derive from the Latin adjective *unus*. Partitive articles, however, derive from Vulgar Latin *de illo*, meaning *(some) of the*.

The English indefinite article *an* is derived from the same root as *one*. The *-n* came to be dropped before consonants, giving rise to the shortened form *a*. The existence of both forms has led to many cases of juncture loss, for example transforming the original *a napron* into the modern *an apron*.

The Persian indefinite article is *yek*, meaning one.

## English articles

The articles in English are the definite article *the* and the indefinite articles *a* and *an*. The term *article* is also used loosely by some scientists to include the determiner *some*. Use of the definite article implies that the speaker assumes the listener knows the identity of the noun's referent (because it is obvious, because it is common knowledge, or because it was mentioned in the same sentence or an earlier sentence). Use of an indefinite article implies that the speaker assumes the listener does not have to be told the identity of the referent. In some noun phrases no article is used.

Articles are a special case of determiners in English; for information about this class as a whole, see English determiners.

## Use of articles

The rules of English grammar require that in most cases a noun, or more generally a noun phrase, must be "completed" with a determiner to clarify what the referent of the noun phrase is. The most common determiners are the articles *the* and *a(n)*, which specify the presence or absence of definiteness of the noun. Other possible determiners include words like *this, my, each* and *many* – see English determiners. There are also cases where no determiner is required, as in the sentence *John likes fast cars*. Or the sentence *Bob likes cool trains*.

The definite article *the* is used when the referent of the noun phrase is assumed to be unique or known from the context. For example, in the sentence *The boy with glasses was looking at the moon*, it is assumed that in the context the reference can only be to one boy and one moon. However, the definite article is *not* used:

- with generic nouns (plural or uncountable): *cars have accelerators, happiness is contagious*, referring to cars in general and happiness in general (compare *the happiness I felt yesterday*, specifying particular happiness);
- with many proper names: *John, France, London*, etc.

The indefinite article *a* (before a consonant sound) or *an* (before a vowel sound) is used only with singular, countable nouns. It indicates that the referent of the noun phrase is one unspecified member of a class. For example, the sentence *An ugly man was smoking a pipe* does not refer to any specifically known ugly man or pipe.

No article is used with plural or uncountable nouns when the referent is indefinite (just as in the generic definite case described above). However, in such situations, the determiner *some* is often added (or *any* in negative contexts and in many questions). For example:

- *There are apples in the kitchen* or *There are some apples in the kitchen;*
- *We do not have information* or *We do not have any information;*
- *Would you like tea?* or *Would you like some tea?* and *Would you like any tea?* or *Would you like some good tea?*

Additionally, articles are not normally used:

- in noun phrases that contain other determiners (*my house, this cat, America's history*), although one can combine articles with certain other determiners, as in *the many issues, such a child.*
- with pronouns (*he, nobody*), although again certain combinations are possible (as *the one, the many, the few*).
- preceding noun phrases consisting of a clause or infinitive phrase (*what you've done is very good, to surrender is to die*).

If it is required to be concise, e. g. in headlines, signs, labels, and notes, articles are often omitted along with certain other function words. For example, rather than *The mayor was attacked*, a newspaper headline might say just *Mayor attacked.*

For more information on article usage, see the sections Definite article and Indefinite article below. For more cases where no article is used, see Zero article in English.

## Word order

In most cases, the article is the first word of its noun phrase, preceding all other adjectives and modifiers.

- *The* little old red bag held *a* very big surprise.

There are a few exceptions, however:

- Certain determiners, such as *all, both, half, double*, precede the definite article when used in combination (*all the team, both the girls, half the time, double the amount*).
- The determiner *such* and exclamative *what* precede the indefinite article (*such an idiot, what a day!*).
- Adjectives qualified by *too, so, as* and *how* generally precede the indefinite article: *too great a loss, so hard a problem, as*

*delicious an apple as I have ever tasted, I know how pretty a girl she is.*

- When adjectives are qualified by *quite* (particularly when it means "fairly"), the word *quite* (but not the adjective itself) often precedes the indefinite article: *quite a long letter.*

## Definite article

"The" redirects here. For other uses, see The (disambiguation).

The only definite article in English is the word ***the***, denoting person(s) or thing(s) already mentioned, under discussion, implied, or otherwise presumed familiar to the listener or reader. *The* is the most commonly used word in the English language, accounting for 7% of all words.

"The" can be used with both singular and plural nouns, with nouns of any gender, and with nouns that start with any letter. This is different from many other languages which have different articles for different genders and/or numbers.

## Pronunciation

In most dialects "the" is pronounced as (with the voiced dental fricative followed by schwa) when followed by a consonant sound. In many dialects, including Received Pronunciation (standard educated speech of England), the pronunciation [ði] is used before words that begin with vowel sounds. The emphatic form of the word is (like *thee*) – see Weak and strong forms in English.

.In some Northern England dialects of English, *the* is pronounced (with a dental t) or as a glottal stop, usually written in eye dialect as; in some dialects it reduces to nothing. This is known as definite article reduction. In dialects that do not have the voiced dental fricative, *the* is pronounced with the voiced dental plosive, as in).

## Etymology

*The* and *that* are common developments from the same Old English system. Old English had a definite article *se*, in the masculine gender, *seo* (feminine), and *þæt* (neuter). In Middle English these had all merged into *þe*, the ancestor of the Modern English word *the*.

## Usage

The principles of the use of the definite article in English are described above under Use of articles. (The word *the* is also used withcomparatives, in phrases like, *the sooner the better*, and, *we were all the happier for it*; this form of the definite article has a somewhat different etymology from other uses of the definite article. (See the Wiktionary entry *the*.)

## Geographical names

An area in which the use or non-use of *the* is sometimes problematic is with geographic names. Names of rivers, seas, mountain ranges, deserts, island groups and the like are generally used with the definite article (*the Rhine, the North Sea, the Alps, the Sahara, the Hebrides*). Names of continents, islands, countries, regions, administrative units, cities and towns mostly do not take the article (*Europe, Skye, Germany, Scandinavia, Yorkshire, Madrid*). However, there are certain exceptions:

- Countries and territories whose names derive from common nouns such as "kingdom", "republic" or even "coast" take the article: *the United States, the United Kingdom, the Soviet Union, the Czech Republic, the Ivory Coast.*
- Countries and territories whose names derive from "island" or "land" however only take the definite article if they represent a plural noun:*The Netherlands* do, *the Falkland Islands, the Faroe Islands* and *the Cayman Islands* do, even *the Philippines* or *the Comoros* do, though the plural noun "Islands" is omitted there. The (singular) *Greenland* on the other hand doesn't take the definite article, neither does*Christmas Island* or *Norfolk Island*.
- Certain countries and regions whose names derive from mountain ranges, rivers, deserts, etc. are sometimes used with an article even though in the singular (*the Lebanon, the Sudan, the Yukon*), but this usage is declining, although The

Gambia remains the recommended name of that country. Since the independence of Ukraine (formerly sometimes called *the Ukraine*), most style guides have advised dropping the article (in some other languages there is a similar issue involving prepositions). Use of *the Argentine* for Argentinais now old-fashioned.

- Some names include an article for historical reasons, such as The Bronx, or to reproduce the native name (The Hague).
- Names beginning with a common noun followed by *of* take the article, as in *the Isle of Wight* or *the Isle of Portland* (compare *Christmas Island*). The same applies to names of institutions: *Cambridge University*, but *the University of Cambridge*.

Abbreviations for "the" and "that" Since "the" is one of the most frequently used words in English, at various times short abbreviations for it have been found:

- Barred thorn: the earliest abbreviation, it is used in manuscripts in the Old English language. It is the letter **þ** with a bold horizontal stroke through the ascender, and it represents the word *þæt*, meaning "the" or "that" (neuter nom. /acc.)
- **þd** and **þm** (þ with a superscript *e* or *t*) appear in Middle English manuscripts for "þe" and "þat" respectively.
- **yd** and **ym** are developed from *þd* and *þm* and appear in Early Modern manuscripts and in print

Occasional proposals have been made by individuals for an abbreviation. In 1916, Legros & Grant included in their classic printers' handbook*Typographical Printing-Surfaces*, a proposal for a letter similar to & to represent "Th", thus abbreviating "the" to 'e. Why they did not propose reintroducing to the English language "*þ*", for which blocks were already available for use in Icelandic texts, or the *yd* form is unknown.

In 2013 an Australian restaurateur named Paul Mathis proposed **Ž**, which he nicknamed "The Tap", as a symbol for "the." This symbol is the same as the Serbian Cyrillic letter Ž (Tshe).

### *Ye* form

In Middle English, *the* (þe) was frequently abbreviated as a *þ* with a small *e* above it, similar to the abbreviation for *that,* which was a *þ* with a small *t* above it. During the latter Middle English and Early Modern English periods, the letter thorn (þ) in its common script, or cursive, form came to resemble a *y* shape. As a result, the use of a *y* with an *e* above it (ẏ) as an abbreviation became common. This can still be seen in reprints of the 1611 edition of the King James Version of the Bible in places such as Romans 15:29, or in the Mayflower Compact. Historically the article was never pronounced with a *y* sound, even when so written.

### Indefinite article

The indefinite article of English takes the two forms *a* and *an*. Semantically they can be regarded as meaning "one", usually without emphasis. They can be used only with singular countable nouns; for the possible use of *some* (or *any*) as an equivalent with plural and uncountable nouns, see Use of *some* below.

### Distinction between *a* and *an*

The form *an* is used before words starting with a vowel sound, regardless of whether the word begins with a vowel letter. This avoids theglottal stop (momentary silent pause) that would otherwise be required between *a* and a following vowel sound. Where the next word begins with a consonant sound, *a* is used. Examples: *a box; an apple; an SSO* (pronounced "es-es-oh"); *a HEPA filter* (HEPA is pronounced as a word rather than as letters); *an hour* (the *h* is silent); *a one-armed bandit* (pronounced "won..."); *an heir* (pronounced "air"); *a unicorn*(pronounced "yoo-"); *an herb* in American English (where the *h* is silent), but *a herb* in British English.

Some speakers and writers use *an* before a word beginning with the sound /h/ in an unstressed syllable: *an historical novel, an hotel*. However, where the "h" is clearly pronounced, this usage is now less common, and "a" is preferred.

Some dialects, particularly in England (such as Cockney), silence many or all initial *h* sounds (h-dropping), and so employ *an* in situations where it would not be used in the standard language, like *an 'elmet* (standard English: *a helmet*).

There used to be a distinction analogous to that between *a* and *an* for the possessive determiners *my* and *thy*, which became *mine* and *thine*before a vowel, as in *mine eyes*.

## In other languages

Other more or less analogous cases in different languages include the Yiddish articles "a" and "an" (used in essentially the same manner as the English ones), the Hungarian articles *a* and *az* (used the same way, except that they are definite articles; juncture loss, as described below, has occurred in that language too), and the privative *a*- and *an*- prefixes, meaning "not" or "without", in Greek and Sanskrit.

## Pronunciation

Both *a* and *an* are usually pronounced with a schwa: /Y/, / Yn/. However, when stressed (which is rare in ordinary speech), they are normally pronounced respectively as /ej/ (to rhyme with *day*) and /æn/ (to rhyme with *pan*). See Weak and strong forms in English.

## Etymology

*An* is the older form (related to *one*, cognate to German *ein*; etc.). *An* was originally an unstressed form of the number *ân* 'one'.

## Usage

The principles for use of the indefinite article are given above under Use of articles.

In addition to serving as an article, *a* and *an* are also used to express a proportional relationship, such as "a dollar a day" or "$150 an ounce" or "A sweet a day helps you work, rest and play", although historically this use of "a" and "an" does not come from the same word as the articles.

## Juncture loss

In a process called juncture loss, the *n* has wandered back and forth between the indefinite article and words beginning with vowels over the history of the language, where for example what was once *a nuncle* is now *an uncle*. The Oxford English Dictionary gives such examples as*smot hym on the hede with a nege tool* from 1448 for *smote him on the head with an edge tool*, as well as *a nox* for *an ox* and *a napple* for*an apple*. Sometimes the change has been permanent. For example, *a newt* was once *an ewt* (earlier *euft* and *eft*), *a nickname* was once *an eke-name*, where *eke* means "extra" (as in *eke out* meaning "add to"), and in the other direction, *a napron* (meaning a little tablecloth, related to the word *napkin*) became *an apron*, and *a naddre* became *an adder*. The initial *n* in orange was also dropped through juncture loss, but this happened before the word was borrowed into English.

## Use of some

The existential determinative (or determiner) *some* is sometimes used as a functional equivalent of *a(n)* with plural and uncountable nouns(also called a partitive). For example, *Give me some apples*, *Give me some water* (equivalent to the singular countable forms *an apple* and *a glass of water*). Grammatically this *some* is not required; it is also possible to use zero article: *Give me apples*, *Give me water*. The use of*some* in such cases implies a more limited quantity. (Compare the forms *unos/unas* in Spanish, which are the plural of the indefinite article*un/una*.) Like the articles, *some* belongs to the class of "central determiners", which are mutually exclusive (so "the some boys" is ungrammatical).

In most negative clauses, and often in questions, the word *any* is used instead of *some*: *Don't give me any apples; Is there any water?*

*Some* can also have a more emphatic meaning: "some but not others" or "some but not many". For example, *some people like football, while others prefer rugby*, or *I've got some money, but not enough to lend you any*. It can also be used as an indefinite pronoun, not qualifying a noun at all (*Give me some!*) or followed by a prepositional phrase (*I want some of your vodka*); the same applies to *any*.

*Some* can also be used with singular countable nouns, as in *There is some person on the porch,* which implies that the identity of the person is unknown to the speaker (which is not necessarily the case when *a(n)* is used). This usage is fairly informal, although singular countable*some* can also be found in formal contexts: *We seek some value of x such that...*

When *some* is used with merely the function of an indefinite article, it is normally pronounced weakly, as [s(Y)m]. In other meanings it is pronounced [sŒm]. See Weak and strong forms in English.

## Effect on alphabetical order

In sorting titles and phrases alphabetically, articles are usually excluded from consideration, since being so common makes them more of a hindrance than a help in finding a desired item. For example, *The Comedy of Errors* is alphabetized before *A Midsummer Night's Dream*, because *the* and *a* are ignored and *comedy* alphabetizes before *midsummer*. In an index, the former work might be written "Comedy of Errors, The", with the article moved to the end.

Common errors in the use of articles

Incorrect: We live **in village.**

Correct: We live **in a village**. OR We live **in the village.**

Incorrect: She works **in pub.**

Correct: She works in **a pub**. OR She works in **the pub.**

A singular common noun (e. g. boy, girl, tree, country, teacher, village etc.) must have an article. A plural common noun can be used with or without an article.

Incorrect: He is **best player** in the team.

Correct: He is **the best player** in the team.

Incorrect: She is **fastest runner**.

Correct: She is **the fastest runner.**

The definite article **the** must be used with superlative adjectives.

Incorrect: **The Paris** is big city.

Correct: **Paris** is a big city.

Incorrect: I live in **the Mumbai.**

Correct: I live **in Mumbai.**

If the noun is proper it will take no article. Note that a proper noun is the name of a particular person, place or thing. Examples are: Sam, Mary, India, Paris, London etc.

Incorrect: **The iron** is a useful metal.

Correct: **Iron** is a useful metal.

Incorrect: **The gold** is yellow.

Correct: **Gold** is yellow.

Articles are not used with material nouns. Examples are: gold, silver, iron, wheat, rice etc.

Incorrect: We should not **make noise.**

Correct: We should not **make a noise.**

Incorrect: I have **an urgent business.**

Correct: I have **urgent business**. OR I have **some urgent business.**

Note these fixed expressions.

Incorrect: Do you sell eggs **by kilo** or **by dozen?**

Correct: Do you sell eggs **by the kilo** or **by the dozen?**

**The** is used in measuring expressions beginning with **by.**

## Chapter-5

# Auxiliary Verbs

An **auxiliary verb** is a verb that adds functional or grammatical meaning to the clause in which it appears—for example, to express tense, aspect, modality, voice, emphasis, etc. Auxiliary verbs usually accompany a main verb. The main verb provides the main semantic content of the clause. An example is the verb *have* in the sentence *I have finished my dinner.* Here, the main verb is *finish,* and the auxiliary *have*helps to express the perfect aspect. Some sentences contain a chain of two or more auxiliary verbs. Auxiliary verbs are also called **helping verbs, helper verbs,** or **(verbal) auxiliaries**. They may be glossed with the abbreviation **AUX**.

### BASIC EXAMPLES

Below are some sentences that contain representative auxiliary verbs from English, German, and French, with the auxiliary verb marked in bold:

a. **Do** you want tea? – *do* is an auxiliary accompanying the main verb *want,* used here to form a question – see *do*-support.

b. He **has** given his all. – *has* is an auxiliary used in expressing the perfect aspect of *give.*

c. Das **wurde** mehrmals gesagt. – *wurde* 'became' is an auxiliary used to build the passive voice in German.

   That became many times said = 'That was said many times.'

d. Sie **ist** nach Hause gegangen. – *ist* 'is' is an auxiliary used with movement verbs to build the perfect tense/aspect in German.
   She is to home gone = 'She went home/She has gone home.'

e. J'**ai** vu le soleil. – *ai* 'have' is an auxiliary used to build the perfect tense/aspect in French.
   I have seen the sun = 'I have seen the sun/I saw the sun.'

f. Nous **sommes** hébergés par un ami. – *sommes* 'are' is an auxiliary used to build the passive voice in French.
   We are hosted by a friend.

These auxiliaries help express a question, show tense/aspect, or form passive voice. Auxiliaries like these typically appear with a full verb that carries the main semantic content of the clause.

## Traits of auxiliary verbs across languages

Auxiliary verbs typically help express grammatical tense, aspect, mood, and voice. They typically appear together with a main verb. The auxiliary is said to "help" the main verb. The auxiliary verbs of a language form a closed class, i. e., there is a fixed, relatively small number of them. They are often among the most frequently occurring verbs in a language.

Widely acknowledged verbs that can serve as auxiliaries in English and many related languages are the equivalents of *be* to express passive voice, and *have* (and sometimes *be*) to express perfect aspect or past time reference.

In some treatments, the copula *be* is classed as an auxiliary even though it does not "help" another verb, e. g.,

The bird **is** in the tree. – *is* serves as a copula with a predicative expression not containing any other verb.

Definitions of auxiliary verbs are not always consistent across languages, or even among authors discussing the same language. Modal verbsmay or may not be classified as auxiliaries, depending on the language. In the case of English, verbs are often identified as auxiliaries based on their grammatical behavior, as described below. In some cases, verbs that function similarly to auxiliaries, but are not considered full members of that class (perhaps because they carry some independent lexical information), are called *semi-auxiliaries*. In French, for example, verbs such as *devoir* (have to), *pouvoir* (be able to), *aller* (be going to), *vouloir* (want), *faire* (make), and *laisser* (let), when used together with the infinitive of another verb, can be called semi-auxiliaries.

## Auxiliary verbs in English

The following sections consider auxiliary verbs in English. They list auxiliary verbs, then present the diagnostics that motivate this special class (subject-auxiliary inversion and negation with *not*). The modal verbs are included in this class, due to their behavior with respect to these diagnostics.

## A list of auxiliaries in English

A list of verbs that (can) function as auxiliaries in English is as follows:

*be* (*am, are, is, was, were, being, been*), *can, could, dare, do* (*does, did*), *have* (*has, had, having*), *may, might, must, need, ought, shall, should, will, would*

The status of *dare, need (not),* and *ought (to)* is debatable. and the use of these verbs as auxiliaries can vary across dialects of English. If the negative forms *can't, don't, won't,* etc. are viewed as separate verbs (and not as contractions), then the number of auxiliaries increases. The verbs *do* and *have* can also function as full verbs or as light verbs, which can be a source of confusion about their status. The modal verbs (*can, could, may, might, must, shall, should, will, would,* and *dare, need* and *ought* when included) form a subclass of auxiliary verbs. Modal verbs are defective insofar as they cannot be inflected, nor do they appear as gerunds, infinitives, or participles.

## Diagnostics for identifying auxiliary verbs in English

The verbs listed in the previous section can be classified as auxiliaries based upon two diagnostics: they allow subject–auxiliary inversion (the type of inversion used to form questions etc.) and (equivalently) they can take *not* as a postdependent (a dependent that follows its head). The following examples illustrate the extent to which subject–auxiliary inversion can occur with an auxiliary verb but not with a full verb:

a. **He was** working today.

b. **Was he** working today? - Auxiliary verb *was* allows subject–auxiliary inversion.

a. **He worked** today.

b. ***Worked he** today? - Full verb *worked* does not allow subject–auxiliary inversion.

a. **She can** see it.

b. **Can she** see it? - Auxiliary verb *can* allows subject–auxiliary inversion.

a. **She sees** it.

b. ***Sees she** it? - Full verb *sees* does not allow subject–auxiliary inversion.

(The asterisk * is the means commonly used in linguistics to indicate that the example is grammatically unacceptable.) The following examples illustrate that the negation *not* can appear as a postdependent of a finite auxiliary verb, but not as a postdependent of a finite full verb:

a. Sam would try that.

b. Sam would **not** try that. - The negation *not* appears as a postdependent of the finite auxiliary *would*.

a. Sam tried that.

b. *Sam tried **not** that. - The negation *not* cannot appear as a postdependent of the finite full verb *tried*.

a. Tom could help.

b. Tom could **not** help. - The negation *not* appears as a postdependent of the finite auxiliary *could*.

a. Tom helped.

b. *Tom helped **not**. - The negation *not* cannot appear as a postdependent of the finite full verb *helped*.

A third diagnostic that can be used for identifying auxiliary verbs is verb phrase ellipsis. Auxiliary verbs can introduce verb phrase ellipsis, but main verbs cannot. See the article on verb phrase ellipsis for examples.

Note that these criteria lead to the copula *be* being considered an auxiliary (it undergoes inversion and takes postdependent *not*, e. g., *Is she the boss?*, *She is not the boss*). However, if one defines *auxiliary verb* as a verb that somehow "helps" another verb, then the copula *be* is not an auxiliary, because it appears without another verb. The literature on auxiliary verbs is somewhat inconsistent in this area.

## Auxiliary verbs vs. light verbs

Some syntacticians distinguish between auxiliary verbs and light verbs. The two are similar insofar as both verb types contribute mainly just functional information to the clauses in which they appear. Hence both do not qualify as separate predicates, but rather they form part of a predicate with another expression - usually with a full verb in the case of auxiliary verbs and usually with a noun in the case of light verbs.

In English, light verbs differ from auxiliary verbs in that they cannot undergo inversion and they cannot take *not* as a postdependent. The verbs *have* and *do* can function as auxiliary verbs or as light verbs (or as full verbs). When they are light verbs, they fail the inversion and negation diagnostics for auxiliaries, e. g.

a. They **had** a long meeting.

b. ***Had** they a long meeting? - Light verb *had* fails the inversion test.

c. *They **had** not a long meeting. - Light verb *had* fails the negation test.

a. She **did** a report on pandering politicians.

b. ***Did** she a report on pandering politicians? - Light verb *did* fails the inversion test.

c. *She **did** not a report on pandering politicians. - Light verb *did* fails the negation test.

(In some cases, though, *have* may undergo auxiliary-type inversion and negation even when it is not used as an auxiliary verb – see Subject–auxiliary inversion: Inversion with other types of verb.)

Sometimes the distinction between auxiliary verbs and light verbs is overlooked or confused. Certain verbs (e. g., *used to, have to,* etc.) may be judged as light verbs by some authors, but as auxiliaries by others.

## Multiple auxiliaries

Most clauses contain at least one main verb, and they can contain zero, one, two, three, or perhaps even more auxiliary verbs. The following example contains three auxiliary verbs and one main verb:

The paper **will have been** scrutinized by Fred.

The auxiliary verbs are in bold and the main verb is underlined. Together these verbs form a verb catena (chain of verbs), i. e., they are linked together in the hierarchy of structure and thus form a single syntactic unit. The main verb *scrutinized* provides the semantic core of sentence meaning, whereby each of the auxiliary verbs contributes some functional meaning. A single finite clause can contain more than three auxiliary verbs, e. g.

Fred **may be being** judged to **have been** deceived by the explanation.

Viewing this sentence as consisting of a single finite clause, there are five auxiliary verbs and two main verbs present. From the point of view of predicates, each of the main verbs constitutes the core of a predicate, and the auxiliary verbs contribute functional meaning to these predicates. These verb catenae are periphrastic forms of English, English being a relatively analytic language. Other languages, such as Latin, are synthetic, which means they tend to express functional meaning with affixes, not with auxiliary verbs.

## Helping and Modal Auxiliary Verbs

**Helping verbs** or **auxiliary verbs** such as *will, shall, may, might, can, could, must, ought to, should, would, used to, need* are used in conjunction with **main verbs** to express shades of time and mood. The combination of helping verbs with main verbs creates what are called **verb phrases** or **verb strings**. In the following sentence, "will have been" are helping or auxiliary verbs and "studying" is the main verb; the whole verb string is underlined:

- As of next August, I will have been studying chemistry for ten years.

Students should remember that adverbs and contracted forms are not, technically, part of the verb. In the sentence, "He has already started." the adverb *already* modifies the verb, but it is not really part of the verb. The same is true of the *'nt* in "He hasn't started yet" (the adverb *not*, represented by the contracted *n't*, is not part of the verb, *has started*).

*Shall, will* and forms of *have, do* and *be* combine with main verbs to indicate time and voice. As auxiliaries, the verbs *be, have* and *do*can change form to indicate changes in subject and time.

- I shall go now.
- He had won the election.
- They did write that novel together.
- I am going now.
- He was winning the election.
- They have been writing that novel for a long time.

Uses of *Shall* and *Will* and *Should*

In England, *shall* is used to express the simple future for first person *I*and *we*, as in "Shall we meet by the river?" *Will* would be used in the simple future for all other persons. Using *will* in the first person would express determination on the part of the speaker, as in "We will finish this project by tonight, by golly!" Using *shall* in second and third persons would indicate some kind of promise about the subject, as in "This shall be revealed to you in good time." This usage is certainly acceptable in the U. S., although *shall*is used far less frequently. The distinction between the two is often obscured by the contraction *'ll*, which is the same for both verbs.

In the United States, we seldom use *shall* for anything other than polite questions (suggesting an element of permission) in the first-person:

- "Shall we go now?"

- "Shall I call a doctor for you?"

(In the second sentence, many writers would use *should* instead, although*should* is somewhat more tentative than *shall.)* In the U. S., to express the future tense, the verb *will* is used in all other cases.

*Shall* is often used in formal situations (legal or legalistic documents, minutes to meetings, etc.) to express obligation, even with third-person and second-person constructions:

- The board of directors shall be responsible for payment to stockholders.
- The college president shall report financial shortfalls to the executive director each semester."

*Should* is usually replaced, nowadays, by *would*. It is still used, however, to mean "ought to" as in

- You really shouldn't do that.
- If you think that was amazing, you should have seen it last night.

In British English and very formal American English, one is apt to hear or read *should* with the first-person pronouns in expressions of liking such as "I should prefer iced tea" and in tentative expressions of opinion such as

- I should imagine they'll vote Conservative.
- I should have thought so.

Uses of *Do, Does* and *Did*

In the simple present tense, *do* will function as an auxiliary **to express the negative and to ask questions**. (*Does*, however, is substituted for third-person, singular subjects in the present tense. The past tense *did* works with all persons, singular and plural.)

- I don't study at night.
- She doesn't work here anymore.
- Do you attend this school?
- Does he work here?

These verbs also work as "short answers," with the main verb omitted.

- Does she work here? No, she doesn't ~~work here~~.

With "yes-no" questions, the form of *do* goes in front of the subject and the main verb comes after the subject:

- Did your grandmother know Truman?
- Do wildflowers grow in your back yard?

Forms of *do* are useful in expressing **similarity and differences** in conjunction with *so* and *neither*.

- My wife hates spinach and so does my son.
- My wife doesn't like spinach; neither do I.

*Do* is also helpful because it means you don't have to repeat the verb:

- Larry excelled in language studies; so did his brother.
- Raoul studies as hard as his sister does.

The so-called *emphatic do* has many uses in English.

a. To add emphasis to an entire sentence: "He does like spinach. He really does!"

b. To add emphasis to an imperative: "Do come in." (actually softens the command)

c. To add emphasis to a frequency adverb: "He never didunderstand his father." "She always does manage to hurt her mother's feelings."

d. To contradict a negative statement: "You didn't do your homework, did you?" "Oh, but I did finish it."

e. To ask a clarifying question about a previous negative statement: "Ridwell didn't take the tools." "Then who did take the tools?"

f. To indicate a strong concession: "Although the Clintons denied any wrong-doing, they did return some of the gifts."

In the absence of other modal auxiliaries, a form of *do* is used in question and negative constructions known as the *get passive*:

- Did Rinaldo get selected by the committee?
- The audience didn't get riled up by the politician.

Uses of *Have, Has* and *Had*

Forms of the verb *to have* are used to create tenses known as the**present perfect** and **past perfect**. The perfect tenses indicate that something has happened in the past; the present perfect indicating that something happened and might be continuing to happen, the past perfect indicating that something happened prior to something else happening. (That sounds worse than it really is!) See the section on **Verb Tenses in the Active Voice** for further explanation; also review material in the **Directory of English Tenses**.

*To have* is also in combination with other modal verbs to express probability and possibility in the past.

- As an affirmative statement, *to have* can express how certain you are that something happened (when combined with an appropriate modal + *have* + a past participle): "Georgia must have left already." "Clinton might have known about the gifts." "They may have voted already."
- As a negative statement, a modal is combined with *not* + *have* + a past participle to express how certain you are that something did not happen: "Clinton might not have known about the gifts." "I may not have been there at the time of the crime."
- To ask about possibility or probability in the past, a modal is combined with the subject + *have* + past participle: "Could Clinton have known about the gifts?"
- For short answers, a modal is combined with *have*: "Did Clinton know about this?" "I don't know. He may have." "The evidence is pretty positive. He must have."

*To have* (sometimes combined with *to get*) is used to express a logical inference:

- It's been raining all week; the basement has to be flooded by now.
- He hit his head on the doorway. He has got to be over seven feet tall!

*Have* is often combined with an infinitive to form an auxiliary whose meaning is similar to "must."

- I have to have a car like that!
- She has to pay her own tuition at college.
- He has to have been the first student to try that.

Modal Auxiliaries

- Other helping verbs, called **modal auxiliaries** or **modals,** such as *can, could, may, might, must, ought to, shall, should, will,* and*would,* do not change form for different subjects. For instance, try substituting any of these modal auxiliaries for *can* with any of the subjects listed below.
- There is also a separate section on the **Modal Auxiliaries**, which divides these verbs into their various meanings of necessity, advice, ability, expectation, permission, possibility, etc., and provides sample sentences in various tenses. See the section on **Conditional Verb Forms** for help with the modal auxiliary *would.* The shades of meaning among modal auxiliaries are multifarious and complex. Most English-as-a-Second-Language textbooks will contain at least one chapter on their usage. For more advanced students, *A University Grammar of English,* by Randolph Quirk and Sidney Greenbaum, contains an excellent, extensive analysis of modal auxiliaries.
- The analysis of **Modal Auxiliaries** is based on a similar analysis in *The Scott, Foresman Handbook for Writers* by Maxine Hairston and John J. Ruszkiewicz. 4th ed. HarperCollins: New York. 1996. The description of helping verbs on this page is based on *The Little, Brown Handbook* by H. Ramsay Fowler and Jane E. Aaron, & Kay Limburg. 6th ed. HarperCollins: New York. 1995. By permission of Addison-Wesley Educational Publishers Inc. Examples in all cases are our own.

## Uses of *Can* and *Could*

**The modal auxiliary *can* is used**

- to express ability (in the sense of being able to do something or knowing how to do something):

  He can speak Spanish but he can't write it very well.
- to expression permission (in the sense of being allowed or permitted to do something):

Can I talk to my friends in the library waiting room? (Note that*can* is less formal than *may*. Also, some writers will object to the use of *can* in this context.)

- to express theoretical possibility:

  American automobile makers can make better cars if they think there's a profit in it.

**The modal auxiliary *could* is used**

- to express an ability in the past:

  I could always beat you at tennis when we were kids.
- to express past or future permission:

  Could I bury my cat in your back yard?
- to express present possibility:

  We could always spend the afternoon just sitting around talking.
- to express possibility or ability in contingent circumstances:

  If he studied harder, he could pass this course.

## Can versus May

Whether the auxiliary verb *can* can be used to express permission or not — "Can I leave the room now?" ["I don't know if you can, but you may."] — depends on the level of formality of your text or situation. As Theodore Bernstein puts it in *The Careful Writer,*"a writer who is attentive to the proprieties will preserve the traditional distinction: *can* for ability or power to do something, *may* for permission to do it.

The question is at what level can you safely ignore the "proprieties." Merriam-Webster's Dictionary, tenth edition, says the battle is over and *can*can be used in virtually any situation to express or ask for permission. Most authorities, however, recommend a stricter adherence to the distinction, at least in formal situations.

Uses of *May* and *Might*

Two of the more troublesome modal auxiliaries are *may* and *might*. When used in the context of granting or seeking permission, *might* is the past tense of *may*. *Might* is considerably more tentative than *may*.

- May I leave class early?
- If I've finished all my work and I'm really quiet, might I leave early?

In the context of expressing possibility, *may* and *might* are interchangeable present and future forms and *might* + *have* + past participle is the past form:

- She might be my advisor next semester.
- She may be my advisor next semester.
- She might have advised me not to take biology.

Avoid confusing the sense of possibility in *may* with the implication of*might*, that a hypothetical situation has not in fact occurred. For instance, let's say there's been a helicopter crash at the airport. In his initial report, before all the facts are gathered, a newscaster could say that the pilot "mayhave been injured." After we discover that the pilot is in fact all right, the newscaster can now say that the pilot "might have been injured" because it is a hypothetical situation that has not occurred. Another example: a body had been identified after much work by a detective. It was reported that "without this painstaking work, the body may have remained unidentified." Since the body was, in fact, identified, *might* is clearly called for.

Uses of *Will* and *Would*

In certain contexts, *will* and *would* are virtually interchangeable, but there are differences. Notice that the contracted form *'ll* is very frequently used for *will*.

*Will* can be used to express willingness:

- I'll wash the dishes if you dry.
- We're going to the movies. Will you join us?

It can also express intention (especially in the first person):

- I'll do my exercises later on.

and prediction:

- specific: The meeting will be over soon.
- timeless: Humidity will ruin my hairdo.
- habitual: The river will overflow its banks every spring.

*Would* can also be used to express willingness:

- Would you please take off your hat?

It can also express insistence (rather rare, and with a strong stress on the word "would"):

- Now you've ruined everything. You *would* act that way.
and characteristic activity:
- customary: After work, he would walk to his home in West Hartford.
- typical (casual): She would cause the whole family to be late, every time.

In a main clause, *would* can express a hypothetical meaning:

- My cocker spaniel would weigh a ton if I let her eat what she wants.

Finally, *would* can express a sense of probability:

- I hear a whistle. That would be the five o'clock train.

Uses of *Used to*

The auxiliary verb construction *used to* is used to express an action that took place in the past, perhaps customarily, but now that action no longer customarily takes place:

- We used to take long vacation trips with the whole family.

The spelling of this verb is a problem for some people because the "-ed" ending quite naturally disappears in speaking: "We yoostoo take long trips." But it ought not to disappear in writing. There are exceptions, though. When the auxiliary is combined with another auxiliary, *did,* the past tense is carried by the new auxiliary and the "-ed" ending is dropped. This will often happen in the interrogative:

- Didn't you use to go jogging every morning before breakfast?
- It didn't use to be that way.

*Used to* can also be used to convey the sense of being accustomed to or familiar with something:

- The tire factory down the road really stinks, but we're used to it by now.
- I like these old sneakers; I'm used to them.

Missing Auxiliaries - Common Errors in English

Not every language uses auxiliary verbs like English. Most Indo-European languages make use of auxiliary verbs, although the characteristics and functions of auxiliary verbs differ from language to language. Other languages replace auxiliary verbs with suffixes added onto the ends of verbs. Missing auxiliaries is therefore a common mistake for non-native English speakers, since many languages either omit auxiliary verbs entirely, or have different usage characteristics.

## Rules and Functions of Auxiliary Verbs

Not every language uses auxiliary verbs like English. Most Indo-European languages make use of auxiliary verbs, although the characteristics and functions of auxiliary verbs differ from language to language. Other languages replace auxiliary verbs with suffixes added onto the ends of verbs. Missing auxiliaries is therefore a common mistake for non-native English speakers, since many languages either omit auxiliary verbs entirely, or have different usage characteristics.

# Chapter-6

# Conditionals

## CONDITIONAL SENTENCE

**Conditional sentences** are sentences expressing factual implications, or hypothetical situations and their consequences. They are so called because the validity of the main clause of the sentence is *conditional* on the existence of certain circumstances, which may be expressed in adependent clause or may be understood from the context.

A full conditional sentence (one which expresses the condition as well as its consequences) therefore contains two clauses: the dependent clause expressing the condition, called the ***protasis***; and the main clause expressing the consequence, called the ***apodosis***. An example of such a sentence (in English) is the following:

If it rains, the picnic will be cancelled.

Here the condition is expressed by the clause "If it rains"; this being the protasis, while the consequence is expressed by "the picnic will be cancelled", this being the apodosis. (The protasis may either precede or follow the apodosis; it is equally possible to say "The picnic will be cancelled if it rains".) In terms of logic, the protasis corresponds to the antecedent, and the apodosis to the consequent.

Languages use a variety of grammatical forms and constructions in conditional sentences. The forms of verbs used in the protasis and apodosis are often subject to particular rules as regards their tense and mood. Many languages have a specialized type of verb form called the conditional mood – broadly equivalent in meaning to the English "would (do something)" – for use in some types of conditional sentence.

## TYPES OF CONDITIONAL SENTENCE

There are various ways of classifying conditional sentences. One distinction is between those that state an implication between facts, and those that set up and refer to a hypothetical situation. There is also the distinction between conditionals that are considered factual or predictive, and those that are considered counterfactual or speculative (referring to a situation that did not or does not really exist).

### Implicative and predictive

A conditional sentence expressing an *implication* (also called a *factual* conditional sentence) essentially states that if one fact holds, then so does another. (If the sentence is not a declarative sentence, then the consequence may be expressed as an order or a question rather than a statement.) The facts are usually stated in whatever grammatical tense is appropriate to them; there are not normally special tense or moodpatterns for this type of conditional sentence. Such sentences may be used to express a certainty, a universal statement, a law of science, etc. (in these cases *if* may often be replaced by *when*):

If you heat water to 100 degrees, it boils.

If the sea is stormy, the waves are high.

They can also be used for logical deductions about particular circumstances (which can be in various mixtures of past, present and future):

If it's raining here now, then it was raining on the West Coast this morning.

If it's raining now, then your laundry is getting wet.

If it's raining now, there will be mushrooms to be picked next week.

If he locked the door, then Kitty is trapped inside.

A *predictive* conditional sentence concerns a situation dependent on a hypothetical (but entirely possible) future event. The consequence is normally also a statement about the future, although it may also be a consequent statement about present or past time (or a question or order).

If I become President, I'll lower taxes.

If it rains this afternoon, everybody will stay home.

If it rains this afternoon, then yesterday's weather forecast was wrong.

If it rains this afternoon, your garden party is doomed.

What will you do if he invites you?

If you see them, shoot!

Counterfactual

In a *counterfactual* or *speculative* conditional sentence, a situation is described as dependent on a condition that is known to be false, or presented as unlikely. The time frame of the hypothetical situation may be past, present or future, and the time frame of the condition does not always correspond to that of the consequence. For example:

If I were king, I could have you thrown in the dungeon.

If I won the lottery, I would buy a car.

If he said that to me, I would run away.

If you had called me, I would have come.

If you had done your job properly, we wouldn't be in this mess now.

The difference in meaning between a "counterfactual" conditional with a future time frame, and a "predictive" conditional as described in the previous section, may be slight. For example, there is no great practical difference in meaning between "If it rained tomorrow, I would cancel the match" and "If it rains tomorrow, I will cancel the match".

It is in the counterfactual type of conditional sentence that the grammatical form called the conditional mood (meaning something like the English "would...") is most often found. For the uses of particular verb forms and grammatical structures in the various types and parts of conditional sentences in certain languages, see the following sections.

## Grammar of conditional sentences

Languages have different rules concerning the grammatical structure of conditional sentences. These may concern the syntactic structure of the condition clause (protasis) and consequence (apodosis), as well as the forms of verbs used in them (particularly their tense and mood). Rules for English and certain other languages are described below; more information can be found in the articles on the grammars of individual languages. (Some languages are also described in the article on the conditional mood.)

## English

In English conditional sentences, the condition clause (protasis) is most commonly introduced by the conjunction *if*, or sometimes other conjunctions or expressions such as *unless*, *provided (that)*, *providing (that)* and *as long as*. Certain condition clauses can also be formulated using inversion without any conjunction (*should you fail...; were he to die...; had they helped us...;* see also the corresponding section about inversion in the English subjunctive article).

In English language teaching, conditional sentences are often classified under the headings **zero conditional, first conditional** (or*conditional I*), **second conditional** (or *conditional II*), **third conditional** (or *conditional III*) and **mixed conditional**, according to the grammatical pattern followed. A range of variations on these structures are possible.

## Zero conditional

"Zero conditional.. refers to conditional sentences that express a simple implication, particularly when both clauses are in the present tense:

If you don't eat for a long time, you become hungry.

This form of the conditional expresses the idea that a universally known fact is being described:

If you touch a flame, you burn yourself.

The act of burning oneself only happens on the condition of the first clause being completed. However such sentences can be formulated with a variety of tenses (and moods), as appropriate to the situation.

## First conditional

"First conditional" refers to predictive conditional sentences; here, normally, the condition is expressed using the present tense and the consequence using the future:

If you make a mistake, someone will let you know.

## Second conditional

"Second conditional" refers to the pattern where the condition clause is in the past tense, and the consequence in conditional mood (using*would* or, in the first person and rarely, *should*). This is used for hypothetical, counterfactual situations in a present or future time frame (where the condition expressed is known to be false or is presented as unlikely).

If I liked parties, I would attend more of them.

If it were to rain tomorrow, I would dance in the street.

The past tense used in the condition clause is historically the past subjunctive; however in modern English this is identical to the pastindicative except in certain dialects in the case of the verb *be* (first and third person singular), where the indicative is *was* and the subjunctive*were*. In this case either form may be used (*was* is more colloquial, and *were* more formal, although the phrase *if I were you* is common in colloquial language too):

If I (he, she, it) was/were rich, there would be plenty of money available for this project.

## Third conditional

"Third conditional" is the pattern where the condition clause is in the past perfect, and the consequence is expressed using the conditional perfect. This is used to refer to hypothetical, counterfactual (or believed likely to be counterfactual) situations in the past

If you had called me, I would have come.

## Mixed conditionals

"Mixed conditional" usually refers to a mixture of the second and third conditionals (the counterfactual patterns). Here either the condition or the consequence, but not both, has a past time reference:

If you had done your job properly, we wouldn't be in this mess now.

If we were soldiers, we wouldn't have done it like that.

Latin

Conditional sentences in Latin are traditionally classified into three categories, based on grammatical structure.

- simple conditions (factual or logical implications)
- present tense [if *present indicative* then *indicative*]
- past tense [if *perfect/imperfect indicative* then *indicative*]
- future conditions
- "future more vivid" [if *future indicative* then *future indicative*]
- "future less vivid" [if *present subjunctive* then *present subjunctive*]
- contrafactual conditions
- "present contrary-to-fact" [if *imperfect subjunctive* then *imperfect subjunctive*]
- "past contrary-to-fact" [if *pluperfect subjunctive* then *pluperfect subjunctive*]

## French

In French, the conjunction corresponding to "if" is *si*. The use of tenses is quite similar to English:

- In implicative conditional sentences, the present tense (or other appropriate tense, mood, etc.) is used in both clauses.
- In predictive conditional sentences, the future tense or imperative generally appears in the main clause, but the condition clause is formed with the present tense (as in English). This contrasts with dependent clauses introduced by certain other conjunctions, such as *quand*("when"), where

French uses the future (while English has the present).

- In counterfactual conditional sentences, the imperfect is used to express the condition (where English similarly uses the past tense). The main clause contains the conditional mood (e. g. *j'arriverais,* "I would arrive").
- In counterfactual conditional sentences with a past time frame, the condition is expressed using the pluperfect e. g. (*s'il avait attendu,* "if he had waited"), and the consequence with the conditional perfect (e. g. *je l'aurais vu,* "I would have seen him"). Again these verb forms parallel those used in English.

As in English, certain mixtures and variations of these patterns are possible.

## Italian

Italian uses the following patterns (the equivalent of "if" is *se*):

- Present tense (or other as appropriate) in both parts of an implicative conditional.
- Future tense in both parts of a predictive conditional sentence (the future is not replaced with the present in condition clauses as in English or French).
- In a counterfactual conditional, the imperfect subjunctive is used for the condition, and the conditional mood for the main clause. A more informal equivalent is to use the imperfect indicative in both parts.
- In a counterfactual conditional with past time frame, the pluperfect subjunctive is used for the condition, and the past conditional (conditional perfect) for the main clause.

## Slavic languages

In Slavic languages, such as Russian, clauses in conditional sentences generally appear in their natural tense (future tense for future reference, etc.) However, for counterfactuals, a conditional/subjunctive marker such as the Russian áû *by* generally appears in both condition and consequent clauses, and this normally accompanies the past tense form of the verb.

See Russian grammar, Bulgarian grammar, etc. for more detail.

## Logic

While the material conditional operator used in logic (i. e.) is sometimes read aloud in the form of a conditional sentence (i. e. "if *p*, then*q*"), the intuitive interpretation of conditional statements in natural language does not always correspond to the definition of this mathematical relation. Modelling the meaning of real conditional statements requires the definition of an indicative conditional, and contrary-to-fact statements require a counterfactual conditional operator, formalized in modal logic.

## CONDITIONAL MOOD

The **conditional mood** is a grammatical mood used to express a proposition whose validity is dependent on some condition, possibly counterfactual. It thus refers to a distinct verb form that expresses a hypothetical state of affairs, or an uncertain event, that is contingent on another set of circumstances. An example of a verb in the conditional mood is the French *aimerait*, meaning "would love" (from the verb *aimer*, "to love").

Conditional mood often refers to an inflected verb form, like the example just given. However the term is also sometimes used in relation to ananalytic construction that performs the same function. Thus a construction like the English *would love* will sometimes be described as representing the conditional mood. In some informal contexts, such as language teaching, it may be called the "conditional tense".

The conditional mood is generally found in the independent clause (*apodosis*) of a conditional sentence, namely the clause that expresses the result of the condition, rather than the dependent clause (*protasis*) expressing the condition. The protasis will often use a different verb form, depending on the grammatical rules of the language in question, such as a past tense form or the subjunctive mood. This is exemplified by the

English sentence "If you loved me you would support me" – here the conditional *would support* appears in the apodosis, while the protasis (the condition clause) uses instead the simple past form *loved*.

Not every conditional sentence involves the conditional mood (and some languages do not have a conditional mood at all). For example, in the sentence "If I win, he will be disappointed", the conditional circumstance is expressed using the future marker *will*. Also a conditional verb form may have other uses besides expressing conditionality; for example the English *would* construction may also be used for past habitual action ("When I was young I would happily walk three miles to school every day"), or with future-in-the-past meaning.

Conditional mood can be denoted by the glossing abbreviation COND. Some languages distinguish more than one conditional mood; the East African language Hadza, for example, has a *potential* conditional expressing possibility, and a *veridical* conditional expressing certainty.

This article describes the formation of the conditional forms of verbs in certain languages. For fuller details of the construction of conditional sentences, see Conditional sentence (and for English specifically, English conditional sentences).

## GERMANIC LANGUAGES

### English

English does not have an inflective (morphological) conditional mood, except in as much as the modal verbs *could, might, should* and *would*may in some contexts be regarded as conditional forms of *can, may, shall* and *will* respectively. What is called the English conditional mood (or just the conditional) is formed periphrastically using the modal verb *would* in combination with the bare infinitive of the main verb. (Occasionally *should* is used in place of *would* with a first person subject – see *shall* and *will*. Also the aforementioned modal verbs *could, might* and *should* may replace *would* in order to express appropriate modality in addition to conditionality.)

English has three types of conditional sentences, which may be described as *factual* ("conditional 0": "When I feel well, I sing"), *predictive*("conditional I": "If I feel well, I will sing"), and *speculative* ("conditional II" or "conditional III": "If I felt well, I would sing" or "If I had felt well, I would have sung"). As in many other languages, it is only the speculative type that causes the conditional mood to be used.

Conditionality may be expressed in several tense–aspect forms. These are the simple conditional (*would sing*), the conditional progressive (*would be singing*), the conditional perfect (*would have sung*), and conditional perfect progressive (*would have been singing*). For the uses of these, see Uses of English verb forms. The conditional simple and progressive may also be called the *present conditional*, while the perfect forms can be called *past conditional.*

For details of the formation of conditional clauses and sentences in English, see English conditional sentences.

## German

In German, two verbal constructions express conditionality:

- *Konjunktiv Futur II* (Konjunktiv II, Futur I) corresponds to English's present conditional. It is formed with the auxiliary verb *werden* in itssubjunctive form, plus the infinitive:

  *Ich würde singen* ("I would sing")

- *Konditional Perfekt* (Konjunktiv II, Futur II) corresponds to English's past conditional. It is a form of the perfect construction: it uses a form of the auxiliary *haben* or *sein* (depending on the main verb) together with the past participle of the main verb. The auxiliary in this case takes past subjunctive form: *hätte/st/t/n* (in the case of *haben*) or *wäre/st/t/n* (in the case of *sein.*

*Ich hätte gesungen* ("I had [subjunctive] sung", i. e. "I would have sung")

*Sie wären gekommen* ("They were [subjunctive] come", i. e. "They would have come")

For more information, see German conjugation.

## Dutch

The main conditional construction in Dutch involves the past tense of the verb *zullen*, the auxiliary of the future tenses, cognate with English*shall*.

*Ik zou zingen* 'I would sing', lit. 'I should sing' — referred to as *onvoltooid verleden toekomende tijd* 'imperfect past future tense'

*Ik zou gegaan zijn* 'I would have gone', lit. 'I should have gone' — referred to as *voltooid verleden toekomende tijd* 'perfect past future tense'

The latter tense is sometimes replaced by the past perfect (*plusquamperfect*).

*Ik was gegaan*, lit. 'I had gone'

## Romance languages

While Latin used the indicative and subjunctive in conditional sentences, most of the Romance languages developed a conditional paradigm. The evolution of these forms (and of the innovative Romance future tense forms) is a well-known example of grammaticalization, whereby a syntactically and semantically independent word becomes a bound morpheme with a highly reduced semantic function. The Romance conditional (and future) forms are derived from the Latin infinitive followed by a finite form of the verb *habçre*. This verb originally meant "own/possess" in Classical Latin, but in Late Latin picked up a grammatical use as a temporal/modal auxiliary. The fixing of word order (infinitive + auxiliary) and the phonological reduction of the inflected forms of *habçre* eventually led to the fusion of the two elements into a single synthetic form.

## Romanian

Romanian uses a periphrastic construction for the conditional, e. g. 1sg *a'*, 2sg *ai*, 3sg/pl *ar*, 1pl *am*, 2pl *ai* + *cânta* 'sing'. The modal clitic mixes forms of Latin *habçre*:

- *ai*, *am*, and *ai* (if not auxiliary clitics) are presumably from the Latin imperfect (**eas, eamus, eatis* < *habçbâs, habçbâmus*, and *habçbâtis*);

- *ar* (< older *arã, are*) allegedly comes from the imperfect subjunctive (3sg *habçret* and 3pl *habçrent*); and
- *a'* (< older *a'i*) continues Latin pluperfect subjunctive *habessim* (cf. Italian impf. subj. *avessi*, French *eusse*) which formed the basis of the Romance imperfect subjunctive

Old Romanian, on the other hand, used a periphrastic construction with the imperfect of *vrea* 'to want' + verb, e. g. *vrea cânta* 'I would sing', *vreai cânta* 'you would sing', etc. Until the 17th century, Old Romanian also preserved a synthetic conditional, e. g. *cântare* 'I would sing' and *darear* 'he would give', retained from either the Latin future perfect or perfect subjunctive (or a mixture of both). Aromanian and Istro-Romanian have maintained the same synthetic conditional:

- Aromanian: *s-cãntárimu* 'I would sing', *s-cãntári('i), s-cãntári, s-cãntárimu, s-cãntáritu, s-cãntári*; and
- Istro-Romanian: *aflår* 'I would find', *aflåri, aflåre, aflårno, aflåritu, aflåru.*

## SLAVIC LANGUAGES

### Russian

In Russian, the conditional mood is formed by the past tense of the verb with the particle áû *by,* which usually follows the verb. For example:

- ß **õîòåë** ïåòü *ja* ***khotél*** *pet'* ("I **wanted** to sing")
- ß **õîòåë áû** ïåòü *ja* ***khotél by*** *pet'* ("I **would like,** *literally* **would want,** to sing")

This form is sometimes also called the subjunctive mood. For more information on its usage, see Russian verbs.

### Polish

Polish forms the conditional (or subjunctive) mood in a similar way to Russian, using the particle *by* together with the past tense of the verb. This is an enclitic particle, which often attaches to the first stressed word in the clause, rather than following the verb. It also takes the personal endings (in the first and second persons) which usually attach to the past tense. For example:

- *œpiewa³em/œpiewa³am* ("I sang", masculine/feminine)
- *œpiewa³(a)**bym***, or *ja **bym** œpiewa³(a)* ("I **would** sing")

There is also a past conditional, which also includes the past tense of the copular verb *byæ*, as in *by³(a)bym œpiewa³(a)* ("I would have sung"), but this is rarely used; the ordinary conditional is normally used instead.

For details see Polish verbs.

## Conditionals

A conditional sentence is a sentence containing the word **if**. There are three basic types of conditional sentence:

1. if clause > present simple tense : main clause > future tense (will)
    - o If you help me, I will help you.
    - o If I win the lottery, I will buy a new car.
    - o If it snows tomorrow, we will go skiing.
2. if clause > past simple tense : main clause > would
    - o If you knew her, you would agree with me.
    - o If I won the lottery, I would buy a new car.
    - o If it snowed tomorrow, we would go skiing.
    - 3. if clause > past perfect tense : main clause > would have
    - o If you had helped me, I would have helped you.
    - o If I had won the lottery, I would have bought a new car.
    - o If it had snowed yesterday, we would have gone skiing.

Of course, it is possible to start conditional sentences with the main clause:

- I will buy a new car if I win the lottery.
- I would buy a new car if I won the lottery.
- I would have bought a new car if I had won the lottery.

English speakers choose one of the three conditional structures as follows:

1. *Condiitional one* - to express a simple statement of fact or intent

- o I will buy a new car if I win the lottery.
- o I will go home if you don't stop criticizing me.
- o You will fail your exams if you don't start working harder.
- o She will lose all her friends if she continues to talk about them behind their backs.

2. *Conditional two* - to refer to a present unreal situation or to a situation in the future that the speaker thinks is unlikely to happen
    - o If I had a lot of money, I would buy a new car. (*but I don't have a lot of money*)
    - o If I were you, I would tell him you're sorry. (*but I am not you*)
    - o If I won the lottery, I would buy a new house. (*but I don't expect to win the lottery*)
    - o If it snowed tomorrow, we would go skiing. (*but I don't have much hope that it will snow*)
3. *Conditional three* - to refer to the past and situations that did not happen
    - o If it had snowed yesterday, we would have gone skiing. (*but it didn't snow, so we didn't go skiing*)
    - o If you had studied harder, you would have passed your test. (*but you didn't study hard, so you didn't pass your test*)
    - o If I had known that, I would have told you. (*but I didn't know, so I didn't tell you*)
    - o If she hadn't been driving slowly, she would have had an accident. (*but she was driving slowly, so she didn't have an accident*)

## Common Errors

In the English language, a **conditional** is a sentence that expresses a condition.

A **condition** is something that must happen before something else can happen.

Conditional sentences commonly begin with words and phrases such as:

- if

- when
- unless
- even if
- only if
- in case

**Examples:**

- You will be allowed to watch television **only if** you finish your homework by 9:00.
- I will be at your wedding tomorrow **unless** my son is still sick.
- **When** the sun sets, the kids will return home.
- **If** you want to be paid for a full day, you have to arrive at work on time.
- **Even if** we leave right now, we will still be late to the wedding.
- Take your cell phone with you **in case** you need to call me.

The four English conditionals are covered in the English Conditionals lesson.

Follow the link and view the **summary table** at the end of the lesson for a quick review.

In this lesson, we will look at the most common errors and tips when using conditionals in modern American English.

The two **most common conditionals** in the English language are the first conditional and second conditional. They can also be called "real" and "unreal" because one will most likely happen in the future, while the other is not likely to happen at all.

## FIRST CONDITIONAL (REAL)

**Structure:**

If + Simple Present, + Will/Won't

OR

**Will/Won't + If + Simple Present**

*Won't = Will + Not

**"**If**" can be replaced with phrases such as:

- even if
- only if
- in case
- unless

This conditional describes things based on **fact**.

We use this conditional when referring to conditions that are **possible** and**very likely** to happen in the future.

Caution!

**The most common mistake is to put will in the conditional clause**. The conditional clause must remain in the simple present tense.

- **Incorrect:**

  Sam won't go to the dance unless you **will** ask him.
- **Correct:**

  Sam won't go to the dance unless you ask him.
- **Incorrect:**

  In case you **will** need my help, I will be in my classroom until 4:00.
- **Correct:**

  In case you need my help, I will be in my classroom until 4:00.
- **Incorrect:**

  Sammy will be allowed to play only if he **will** share his toys.
- **Correct:**

  Sammy will be allowed to play only if he shares his toys.
- **Incorrect:**

  If you **will** eat your vegetables, you will be allowed to watch television.
- **Correct:**

  If you eat your vegetables, you will be allowed to watch television.

## Second conditional (unreal)

Structure:

If + Simple Past, + Would/Wouldn't + Base Form
OR
Would/Wouldn't + Base Form + If + Simple Past
*Wouldn't = Would + Not
**"**If**" can be replaced with phrases such as:

- even if
- only if
- in case

This conditional describes **unreal** or **imaginary conditions.**

We use this conditional when referring to conditions that are **not likely** to happen or contrary to present facts.

Caution!

**The most common mistake in second conditional is putting would in the conditional clause.** The conditional clause must be written in the simple past tense.

- **Incorrect:**

If I **would** win the big prize, I would take you to dinner at a fancy restaurant.

- **Correct:**

If I won the big prize, I would take you to dinner at a fancy restaurant.

- **Incorrect:**

She would go to Spain only if her parents **would** buy her a plane ticket.

- **Correct:**

She would go to Spain only if her parents bought her a plane ticket.

- **Incorrect:**

Tom wouldn't like broccoli even if you **would** cover it in cheese.

- **Correct:**

Tom wouldn't like broccoli even if you covered it in cheese.

- **Incorrect:**

I would be the happiest boy alive if I **would** have a monkey for a pet.

- **Correct:**

  I would be the happiest boy alive if I had a monkey for a pet.

## Third conditional (past)

Structure:

If + Past Perfect, + Would/Wouldn't have + V3

OR

Would/Wouldn't have + V3 + If + Past Perfect

**Wouldn't = Would + Not

**"**If**" can be replaced with phrases such as:

- even if
- only if

This conditional refers to things that happened in the **past** and are**impossible to change**.

Caution!

Like the second conditional, **the most common mistake for third conditional is putting would in the conditional clause**.

- **Incorrect:**

  If you **would** have remembered your list, you would have known what to buy at the store.

- **Correct:**

  If you had remembered your list, you would have known what to buy at the store.

- **Incorrect:**

  Richard would have shoveled the sidewalk only if he **would** have known you were arriving.

- **Correct:**

  Richard would have shoveled the sidewalk only if he had known you were arriving.

- **Incorrect:**

  The students wouldn't have finished their work even if the teacher**would** have been there.

- **Correct:**

  The students wouldn't have finished their work even if the teacher had been there.

- **Incorrect:**

  If she had **would** have filled the car up with gas, she would not have been late.

  Correct:

  If she had filled the car up with gas, she would not have been late.

## Zero conditional (always true)

Structure:

If/When + Simple Present + Simple Present

OR

**Simple Present + If/When + Simple Present**

This type of conditional is **almost always true** and is in the simple present tense, meaning it **can happen any time**.

Caution!

The most common mistake is to use will in the main clause.

- **Incorrect:**

  When you leave the milk out, it **will** become sour.
- **Correct:**

  When you leave the milk out, it becomes sour.
- **Incorrect:**

  If it is cold inside, the heater **will** turn on.
- **Correct:**

  If it is cold inside, the heater turns on.
- **Incorrect:**

  Nick **will** need medicine if he coughs.
- **Correct:**

  Nick needs medicine if he coughs.

  Conditionals in English – tips for commas

1. When the condition comes first, a comma is usually used after the conditional.

   **Examples:**

- If Tommy eats his vegetables, he will be allowed to eat dessert.

- Even if Mom picks me up by 4:30, I won't have time to come to your house before practice.
- If Sally is sick, she must stay home.
- Unless you finish your degree in education, you cannot be hired as a certified teacher.
- When you leave the dog in the house, he tears up the furniture.

2. When the condition comes second, no comma is needed.

**Examples:**

- You will be allowed to listen to music during class if you promise to complete your work.
- Turn off the computer when you are finished.
- Jill will go to the dance with him only if he asks her.
- You won't pass this class unless you study.
- The rain will turn into snow unless the temperature rises soon.

Chapter-7

# Conjunctions

## CONJUNCTION (GRAMMAR)

"But" redirects here. For other uses, see BUT.

Not to be confused with conjugation (grammar).

In grammar, a **conjunction** (abbreviated CONJ or CNJ) is a part of speech that connects words, sentences, phrases, or clauses. A *discourse connective* is a conjunction joining sentences. This definition may overlap with that of other parts of speech, so what constitutes a "conjunction" must be defined for each language. In general, a conjunction is an invariable grammatical particle, and it may or may not stand between the items it conjoins.

The definition may also be extended to idiomatic phrases that behave as a unit with the same function, e. g."as well as", "provided that".

A simple literary example of a conjunction: "the truth of nature, *and* the power of giving interest" (Samuel Taylor Coleridge's *Biographia Literaria*)

Conjunctions may be placed at the beginning of sentences. But some superstition about the practice persists.

### Coordinating conjunctions

**Coordinating conjunctions**, also called **coordinators**, are conjunctions that join, or coordinate, two or more items (such as words, main clauses, or sentences) of equal syntactic importance. In English, the mnemonic acronym *FANBOYS* can be used to remember the coordinators*for, and, nor, but, or, yet,* and *so*. These are not the only coordinating conjunctions; various others are used, including"and nor" (British), "but nor" (British), "or nor" (British), "neither" ("They don't gamble; neither do they smoke"), "no more" ("They don't gamble; no more do they smoke"), and "only" ("I would go, only I don't have time"). Types of coordinating conjunctions include cumulative conjunctions, adversative conjunctions, alternative conjunctions, and illative conjunctions.

Here are some examples of coordinating conjunctions in English and what they do:

### For

presents rationale ("They do not gamble or smoke, for they are ascetics.")

### And

presents non-contrasting item(s) or idea(s) ("They gamble and they smoke.")

### Nor

presents a non-contrasting negative idea ("They do not gamble, nor do they smoke.")

### But

presents a contrast or exception ("They gamble, but they don't smoke.")

### Or

presents an alternative item or idea ("Every day they gamble or they smoke.")

### Yet

presents a contrast or exception ("They gamble, yet they don't smoke.")

## So

presents a consequence ("He gambled well last night so he smoked a cigar to celebrate.")

## Correlative conjunctions

**Correlative conjunctions** work in pairs to join words and groups of words of equal weight in a sentence. There are many different pairs of correlative conjunctions:

1. either... or
2. not only... but (also)
3. may... but
4. neither... nor
5. both... and
6. whether... or
7. just as... so
8. the... the
9. as... as
10. as much... as
11. no sooner... than
12. rather... than

Examples:

- You **either** do your work **or** prepare for a trip to the office. (Either do, or prepare)
- He is **not only** handsome, **but also** brilliant. (Not only A, but also B)
- **Not only** is he handsome, **but also** he is brilliant. (Not only is he A, but also he is B.)
- He **may** be tired from sleep, **but** he still needs to work.
- **Neither** the basketball team **nor** the football team is doing well.
- **Both** the cross country team **and** the swimming team are doing well.
- You must decide **whether** you stay **or** you go. (It's up to you)
- **Whether** you stay **or** you go, the film must start at 8 pm. (It's not up to you)

- **Just as** many Americans love basketball, **so** many Canadians love ice hockey.
- **The** more you practice dribbling, **the** better you will be at it.
- Football is **as** fast **as** hockey (is (fast)).
- Football is **as much** an addiction **as** a sport.
- **No sooner** did she learn to ski, **than** the snow began to thaw.
- I would **rather** swim **than** surf.

Subordinating conjunctions

**Subordinating conjunctions**, also called **subordinators**, are conjunctions that join an independent clause and a dependent clause, and also introduce adverb clauses. The most common subordinating conjunctions in the English language include *after, although, as, as far as, as if, as long as, as soon as, as though, because, before, even if, even though, every time, if, in order that, since, so, so that, than, though, unless, until, when, whenever, where, whereas, wherever,* and *while.*

Complementizers can be considered to be special subordinating conjunctions that introduce complement clauses: e. g. "I wonder *whether* he'll be late. I hope *that* he'll be on time". Some subordinating conjunctions (*until* and *while*), when used to introduce a phrase instead of a full clause, become prepositions with identical meanings.

The subordinating conjunction performs two important functions within a sentence: illustrating the importance of the independent clause and providing a transition between two ideas in the same sentence by indicating a time, place, or cause and therefore effecting the relationship between the clauses.

In many verb-final languages, subordinate clauses must precede the main clause on which they depend. The equivalents to the subordinating conjunctions of non-verb-final languages such as English are either

- clause-final conjunctions (e. g. in Japanese); or
- suffixes attached to the verb, and not separate words

Such languages often lack conjunctions as a part of speech, because:

1. the form of the verb used is formally nominalised and cannot occur in an independent clause
2. the clause-final conjunction or suffix attached to the verb is a marker of case and is also used in nouns to indicate certain functions. In this sense, the subordinate clauses of these languages have much in common with postpositional phrases.

In other West Germanic languages like German and Dutch, the word order after a subordinating conjunction is different from that in an independent clause, e. g. in Dutch *want* ("for") is coordinating, but *omdat* ("because") is subordinating. The clause after the coordinating conjunction has normal word order, but the clause after the subordinating conjunction has verb-final word order. Compare:

Hij gaat naar huis, **want** hij **is** ziek. ("He goes home, for he is ill.")

Hij gaat naar huis, **omdat** hij ziek **is**. ("He goes home, because he is ill.")

Similarly, in German, "denn" (for) is coordinating, but "weil" (because) is subordinating:

Er geht nach Hause, **denn** er **ist** krank. ("He goes home, for he is ill.")

Er geht nach Hause, **weil** er krank **ist**. ("He goes home, because he is ill.")

## Starting a sentence

Many students are taught, and one guide maintains, that English sentences should not start with conjunctions such as "and", "but", "because", and "so". Some hypothesize that teachers invented this "rule" to encourage students to avoid overly simple sentences. This superstition has "no historical or grammatical foundation". First-rate writers from across the English-speaking world regularly begin sentences with conjunctions, in even the most formal writing:

- "But she must give security that she will not marry without royal consent, if she holds her lands of the Crown, or without the consent of whatever other lord she may hold them of."

- "But we, or our chief justice if we are not in England, are first to be informed."
- "So please you, step aside."
- "Yet, if thou swear'st, Thou mayst prove false."
- "And for the support of this Declaration, with a firm reliance on the protection of divine Providence, we mutually pledge to each other our Lives, our Fortunes and our sacred Honor."
- "But in all such Cases the Votes of both Houses shall be determined by Yeas and Nays, and the Names of the Persons voting for and against the Bill shall be entered on the Journal of each House respectively."
- "But in chusing the President, the Votes shall be taken by States, the Representatives from each State having one Vote; a quorum for this Purpose shall consist of a Member or Members from two thirds of the States, and a Majority of all the States shall be necessary to a Choice."
- "And the Congress may by general Laws prescribe the Manner in which such Acts, Records and Proceedings shall be proved, and the Effect thereof."
- "And they shall make a List of all the Persons voted for, and of the Number of Votes for each; which List they shall sign and certify, and transmit sealed to the Seat of the Government of the United States, directed to the President of the Senate."
- "And this power has been exercised when the last act, required from the person possessing the power, has been performed."
- "But, in a larger sense, we can not dedicate, we can not consecrate, we can not hallow this ground."
- "Yet, if God wills that it continue until all the wealth piled by the bondsman's two hundred and fifty years of unrequited toil shall be sunk, and until every drop of blood drawn with the lash shall be paid by another drawn with the sword, as was said three thousand years ago, so still it must be said "the judgments of the Lord are true and righteous altogether."

- "So he took him to his own house, and dressed him up clean and nice, and had him to breakfast and dinner and supper with the family, and was just old pie to him, so to speak."
- "And after supper he talked to him about temperance and such things till the old man cried, and said he'd been a fool, and fooled away his life; but now he was a-going to turn over a new leaf and be a man nobody wouldn't be ashamed of, and he hoped the judge would help him and not look down on him."
- "Because no man can ever feel his own identity aright except his eyes be closed; as if darkness were indeed the proper element of our essences, though light be more congenial to our clayey part."
- "Because, while the whales of this order, though smaller than those of the former order, nevertheless retain a proportionate likeness to them in figure, yet the bookbinder's Quarto volume in its dimensioned form does not preserve the shape of the Folio volume, but the Octavo volume does."
- "So the inquiries can coexist, though there is much overlap between them."
- "And it appears that it was this latter factor which underlay the dismissal of the appeal by the majority. But it seems to me that the question of whether it is fair, just and reasonable is better considered against the background of whether a sufficiently proximate relationship exists."
- "But the earlier decisions in Pratap Narain Singh Deo and Valsala K. were not brought to the notice of the Court in the two later decisions in Mubasir Ahmed and Mohd. Nasir."
- "And now we have Facebook and Twitter and Wordpress and Tumblr and all those other platforms that take our daily doings and transform them into media."
- "So any modern editor who is not paranoid is a fool".
- "Because, in the end, free markets and free minds will win".
- "And strikes are protected globally, existing in many of the countries with labour laws outside the Wagner Act model."

## Conjunctive adverb

A **conjunctive adverb** is an adverb that connects two independent clauses. Conjunctive adverbs show cause and effect, sequence, contrast, comparison, or other relationships. The adverbs and adverbial phrases that fit the criteria for a conjunctive adverb are always modifiers of the predicate in the first independent clause.

Conjunctive adverbs can only be used to connect independent clauses, and are one of several methods of doing so. Conjunctive adverbs also do not exclude the possibility of having a dependent clause making a compound-complex sentence. As with other types of adverbs, conjunctive adverbs may be moved within the sentence or clause they appear in.

## Common conjunctive adverbs

- certainly
- comparatively
- consequently
- contrarily
- conversely
- elsewhere
- equally
- eventually
- finally
- further
- furthermore
- hence
- henceforth
- however
- in addition
- in comparison
- in contrast
- in fact
- incidentally
- indeed

- instead
- just as
- likewise
- meanwhile
- moreover
- namely
- nevertheless
- next
- nonetheless
- notably
- now
- otherwise
- rather
- similarly
- still
- subsequently
- that is
- then
- thereafter
- therefore
- thus
- undoubtedly
- uniquely
- whereas
- on the other hand

Many common examples listed above are of adverbial phrases, particularly containing prepositions, that are not exclusively a single conjunctive adverb; however, its function and mechanics are identical.

## Punctuation

The following rules are considered to be correct punctuation for conjunctive adverbs:

- If a conjunctive adverb is used wisely, the independent clauses must be joined by a semicolon followed by the verb.

- After a conjunctive adverb must be a comma which precedes the second independent clause being connected.

Like other adverbs, conjunctive adverbs may move around in the clause (or sentence) in which they appear. When they appear at the end of the clause, they are preceded by a comma.

## Examples

The sentences in question are using an independent clause, follow by a semicolon, the conjunctive adverb, then a comma and the second independent clause.

- He can leap tall buildings in a single bound; furthermore, Dwight is a hog.
- Bret enjoys video games; therefore, he is a crazy nerd.
- He went to the store; however, he did not buy anything.
- Stephanie lent me a barrel of pickled plums; consequently, she is my girlfriend.
- I sat down alongside Adam. Thereafter, he sang.
- Elaine wanted to high-five the friendly giant; consequently, she had to jump to reach him.
- Jade was talking in class; therefore, she got in trouble.

## Conjunctions Definition

Some words are satisfied spending an evening at home, alone, eating ice-cream right out of the box, watching *Seinfeld* re-runs on TV, or reading a good book. Others aren't happy unless they're out on the town, mixing it up with other words; they're *joiners* and they just can't help themselves. **A conjunction is a joiner, a word that connects (conjoins) parts of a sentence.**

### COORDINATING CONJUNCTIONS

The simple, little conjunctions are called **coordinating conjunctions** (you can click on the words to see specific descriptions of each one):

| Coordinating Conjunctions | | | | | | |
|---|---|---|---|---|---|---|
| and | but | or | yet | for | nor | so |

(It may help you remember these conjunctions by recalling that they all have fewer than four letters. Also, remember the acronymFANBOYS: For-And-Nor-But-Or-Yet-So. Be careful of the words then and now; neither is a coordinating conjunction, so what we say about coordinating conjunctions' roles in a sentence and punctuation does not apply to those two words.)

When a coordinating conjunction connects two **independent clauses**, it is often (but not always) accompanied by a comma:

- Ulysses wants to play for UConn, but he has had trouble meeting the academic requirements.

When the two independent clauses connected by a coordinating conjunction are nicely balanced or brief, many writers will omit the comma:

- Ulysses has a great jump shot but he isn't quick on his feet.

The comma is always correct when used to separate two independent clauses connected by a coordinating conjunction. See **Punctuation Between Two Independent Clauses** for further help.

A comma is also correct when *and* is used to attach the last item of a serial list, although many writers (especially in newspapers) will omit that final comma:

- Ulysses spent his summer studying basic math, writing, and reading comprehension.

When a coordinating conjunction is used to connect all the elements in a series, a comma is not used:

- Presbyterians and Methodists and Baptists are the prevalent Protestant congregations in Oklahoma.

A comma is also used with *but* when expressing a contrast:

- This is a useful rule, but difficult to remember.

In most of their other roles as joiners (other than joining independent clauses, that is), coordinating conjunctions can join two sentence elements without the help of a comma.

- Hemingway and Fitzgerald are among the American expatriates of the between-the-wars era.
- Hemingway was renowned for his clear style and his insights into American notions of male identity.
- It is hard to say whether Hemingway or Fitzgerald is the more interesting cultural icon of his day.
- Although Hemingway is sometimes disparaged for his unpleasant portrayal of women and for his glorification of *machismo,* we nonetheless find some sympathetic, even heroic, female figures in his novels and short stories.

## BEGINNING A SENTENCE WITH *AND* OR *BUT*

A frequently asked question about conjunctions is whether *and* or *but* can be used at the beginning of a sentence. This is what R. W. Burchfield has to say about this use of *and*:

There is a persistent belief that it is improper to begin a sentence with *And,* but this prohibition has been cheerfully ignored by standard authors from Anglo-Saxon times onwards. An initial *And* is a useful aid to writers as the narrative continues.

from *The New Fowler's Modern English Usage* edited by R. W. Burchfield. Clarendon Press: Oxford, England. 1996. Used with the permission of Oxford University Press.

The same is true with the conjunction *but.* A sentence beginning with *and* or *but* will tend to draw attention to itself and its transitional function. Writers should examine such sentences with two questions in mind: (1) would the sentence and paragraph function just as well without the initial conjunction? (2) should the sentence in question be connected to the previous sentence? If the initial conjunction still seems appropriate, use it.

Among the coordinating conjunctions, the most common, of course, are *and, but,* and *or.* It might be helpful to explore the uses of these three little words. The examples below by no means exhaust the possible meanings of these conjunctions.

## AND

a. To suggest that one idea is chronologically sequential to another: "Tashonda sent in her applications and waited by the phone for a response."

b. To suggest that one idea is the result of another: "Willie heard the weather report and promptly boarded up his house."

c. To suggest that one idea is in contrast to another (frequently replaced by *but* in this usage): "Juanita is brilliant and Shalimar has a pleasant personality.

d. To suggest an element of surprise (sometimes replaced by *yet* in this usage): "Hartford is a rich city and suffers from many symptoms of urban blight."

e. To suggest that one clause is dependent upon another, conditionally (usually the first clause is an imperative): "Use your credit cards frequently and you'll soon find yourself deep in debt."

f. To suggest a kind of "comment" on the first clause: "Charlie became addicted to gambling — and that surprised no one who knew him."

## BUT

a. To suggest a contrast that is unexpected in light of the first clause: "Joey lost a fortune in the stock market, but he still seems able to live quite comfortably."

b. To suggest in an affirmative sense what the first part of the sentence implied in a negative way (sometimes replaced by *on the contrary*): "The club never invested foolishly, but used the services of a sage investment counselor."

c. To connect two ideas with the meaning of "with the exception of" (and then the second word takes over as subject): "Everybodybut Goldenbreath is trying out for the team."

## OR

a. To suggest that only one possibility can be realized, excluding one or the other: "You can study hard for this exam or you can fail."

b. To suggest the inclusive combination of alternatives: "We can broil chicken on the grill tonight, or we can just eat leftovers.

c. To suggest a refinement of the first clause: "Smith College is the premier all-women's college in the country, or so it seems to most Smith College alumnae."

d. To suggest a restatement or "correction" of the first part of the sentence: "There are no rattlesnakes in this canyon, or so our guide tells us."

e. To suggest a negative condition: "The New Hampshire state motto is the rather grim "Live free or die."

f. To suggest a negative alternative without the use of an imperative : "They must approve his political style or they wouldn't keep electing him mayor."

Authority used for this section on the uses of *and, but,* and *or*: *A University Grammar of English* by Randolph Quirk and Sidney Greenbaum. Longman Group: Essex, England. 1993. Used with permission. Examples our own.

**The Others...**

The conjunction ***NOR*** is not extinct, but it is not used nearly as often as the other conjunctions, so it might feel a bit odd when *nor* does come up in conversation or writing. Its most common use is as the little brother in the correlative pair, *neither-nor*:

- He is neither sane nor brilliant.
- That is neither what I said nor what I meant.

>It can be used with other negative expressions:

- That is not what I meant to say, nor should you interpret my statement as an admission of guilt.

It is possible to use *nor* without a preceding negative element, but it is unusual and, to an extent, rather stuffy:

- George's handshake is as good as any written contract, nor has he ever proven untrustworthy.

The word ***YET*** functions sometimes as an adverb and has several meanings: in addition ("yet another cause of trouble" or "a simple yet noble woman"), even ("yet more expensive"), still ("he is yet a novice"), eventually ("they may yet win"), and so soon as now ("he's not here yet"). It also functions as a coordinating conjunction meaning something like "nevertheless" or "but." The word *yet* seems to carry an element of distinctiveness that *but* can seldom register.

- John plays basketball well, yet his favorite sport is badminton.
- The visitors complained loudly about the heat, yet they continued to play golf every day.

In sentences such as the second one, above, the pronoun subject of the second clause ("they," in this case) is often left out. When that happens, the comma preceding the conjunction might also disappear: "The visitors complained loudly yet continued to play golf every day."

*Yet* is sometimes combined with other conjunctions, *but* or *and*. It would not be unusual to see and yet in sentences like the ones above. This usage is acceptable.

The word *FOR* is most often used as a preposition, of course, but it does serve, on rare occasions, as a coordinating conjunction. Some people regard the conjunction for as rather highfalutin and literary, and it does tend to add a bit of weightiness to the text. Beginning a sentence with the conjunction "for" is probably not a good idea, except when you're singing "For he's a jolly good fellow. "For" has serious sequential implications and in its use the order of thoughts is more important than it is, say, with *because* or *since*. Its function is to introduce the reason for the preceding clause:

- John thought he had a good chance to get the job, for his father was on the company's board of trustees.
- Most of the visitors were happy just sitting around in the shade, for it had been a long, dusty journey on the train.

Be careful of the conjunction *SO*. Sometimes it can connect two independent clauses along with a comma, but sometimes it can't. For instance, in this sentence,

- Soto is not the only Olympic athlete in his family, so are his brother, sister, and his Uncle Chet.

where the word *so* means "as well" or "in addition," most careful writers would use a semicolon between the two independent clauses. In the following sentence, where *so* is acting like a minor-league "therefore," the conjunction and the comma are adequate to the task:

- Soto has always been nervous in large gatherings, so it is no surprise that he avoids crowds of his adoring fans.

Sometimes, at the beginning of a sentence, *so* will act as a kind of summing up device or transition, and when it does, it is often set off from the rest of the sentence with a comma:

- So, the sheriff peremptorily removed the child from the custody of his parents.

## The Case of Then and Than

In some parts of the United States, we are told, *then* and *than* not only look alike, they sound alike. Like a teacher with twins in her classroom, you need to be able to distinguish between these two words; otherwise, they'll become mischievous. They are often used and they should be used for the right purposes.

*Than* is used to make comparisons. In the sentence "Piggy would rather be rescued then stay on the island," we have employed the wrong word because a comparison is being made between Piggy's two choices; we need *than* instead. In the sentence, "Other than *Pincher Martin,* Golding did not write another popular novel," the adverbial construction "other than" helps us make an implied comparison; this usage is perfectly acceptable in the United States but careful writers in the UK try to avoid it (Burchfield).

Generally, the only question about *than* arises when we have to decide whether the word is being used as a conjunction or as a preposition. If it's a preposition (and Merriam-Webster's dictionary provides for this usage), then the word that follows it should be in the object form.

- He's taller and somewhat more handsome than me.

- Just because you look like him doesn't mean you can play better than him.

Most careful writers, however, will insist that *than* be used as a conjunction; it's as if part of the clause introduced by *than* has been left out:

- He's taller and somewhat more handsome than I [am handsome].
- You can play better than he [can play].

In formal, academic text, you should probably use *than* as a conjunction and follow it with the subject form of a pronoun (where a pronoun is appropriate).

*Then* is a conjunction, but it is not one of the little conjunctions listed at the top of this page. We can use the **FANBOYS** conjunctions to connect two independent clauses; usually, they will be accompanied (preceded) by a comma. Too many students think that *then* works the same way: "Caesar invaded Gaul, then he turned his attention to England." You can tell the difference between *then* and a coordinating conjunction by trying to move the word around in the sentence. We can write "he then turned his attention to England"; "he turned his attention, then, to England"; he turned his attention to England then." The word can move around within the clause. Try that with a conjunction, and you will quickly see that the conjunction cannot move around. "Caesar invaded Gaul, and then he turned his attention to England." The word *and* is stuck exactly there and cannot move like *then*, which is more like an adverbial conjunction (or conjunctive adverb — see below) than a coordinating conjunction. Our original sentence in this paragraph — "Caesar invaded Gaul, then he turned his attention to England" — is a **comma splice**, a faulty sentence construction in which a comma tries to hold together two independent clauses all by itself: the comma needs a coordinating conjunction to help out, and the word*then* simply doesn't work that way.

## Subordinating Conjunctions

A **Subordinating Conjunction** (sometimes called a dependent word or subordinator) comes at the beginning of a

**Subordinate (or Dependent) Clause** and establishes the relationship between the dependent clause and the rest of the sentence. It also turns the clause into something that depends on the rest of the sentence for its meaning.

- He took to the stage as though he had been preparing for this moment all his life.
- Because he loved acting, he refused to give up his dream of being in the movies.
- Unless we act now, all is lost.

Notice that some of the subordinating conjunctions in the table below — after, before, since — are also prepositions, but as subordinators they are being used to introduce a clause and to subordinate the following clause to the independent element in the sentence.

### COMMON SUBORDINATING CONJUNCTIONS

| | | |
|---|---|---|
| after | if | though |
| although | if only | till |
| as | in order that | unless |
| as if | now that | until |
| as long as | once | when |
| as though | rather than | whenever |
| because | since | where |
| before | so that | whereas |
| even if | than | wherever |
| even though | that | while |

## The Case of Like and As

Strictly speaking, the word *like* is a preposition, not a conjunction. It can, therefore, be used to introduce a prepositional phrase ("My brother is tall like my father"), but it should not be used to introduce a clause ("My brother can't play the piano ~~like~~ as he did before the accident" or "It looks ~~like~~ as if basketball is quickly overtaking baseball as America's national sport."). To introduce a clause, it's a good idea to use*as*, *as though*, or *as if*, instead.

- ~~Like~~ As I told you earlier, the lecture has been postponed.
- It looks ~~like~~ as if it's going to snow this afternoon.
- Johnson kept looking out the window ~~like~~ as though he had someone waiting for him.

In formal, academic text, it's a good idea to reserve the use of *like* for situations in which similarities are being pointed out:

- This community college is like a two-year liberal arts college.

However, when you are listing things that have similarities, *such as* is probably more suitable:

- The college has several highly regarded neighbors, ~~like~~ such as the Mark Twain House, St. Francis Hospital, the Connecticut Historical Society, and the UConn Law School.

## Omitting *That*

The word *that* is used as a conjunction to connect a subordinate clause to a preceding verb. In this construction *that* is sometimes called the "expletive *that*." Indeed, the word is often omitted to good effect, but the very fact of easy omission causes some editors to take out the red pen and strike out the conjunction *that* wherever it appears. In the following sentences, we can happily omit the *that* (or keep it, depending on how the sentence sounds to us):

- Isabel knew [that] she was about to be fired.
- She definitely felt [that] her fellow employees hadn't supported her.
- I hope [that] she doesn't blame me.

Sometimes omitting the *that* creates a break in the flow of a sentence, a break that can be adequately bridged with the use of a comma:

- The problem is, ~~that~~ production in her department has dropped.
- Remember, ~~that~~ we didn't have these problems before she started working here.

As a general rule, if the sentence feels just as good without the *that*, if no ambiguity results from its omission, if the sentence is more efficient or elegant without it, then we can safely omit the *that*. Theodore Bernstein lists three conditions in which we should maintain the conjunction *that*:

- When a time element intervenes between the verb and the clause: "The boss said yesterday thatproduction in this department was down fifty percent." (Notice the position of "yesterday.")
- When the verb of the clause is long delayed: "Our annual report revealed that some losses sustained by this department in the third quarter of last year were worse than previously thought." (Notice the distance between the subject "losses" and its verb, "were.")
- When a second *that* can clear up who said or did what: "The CEO said that Isabel's department was slacking off and that production dropped precipitously in the fourth quarter." (Did the CEO say that production dropped or was the drop a result of what he said about Isabel's department? The second *that*makes the sentence clear.)

## Beginning a Sentence with Because

Somehow, the notion that one should not begin a sentence with the subordinating conjunction *because*retains a mysterious grip on people's sense of writing proprieties. This might come about because a sentence that begins with *because* could well end up a fragment if one is not careful to follow up the "because clause" with an independent clause.

- Because e-mail now plays such a huge role in our communications industry.

When the "because clause" is properly subordinated to another idea (regardless of the position of the clause in the sentence), there is absolutely nothing wrong with it:

- Because e-mail now plays such a huge role in our communications industry, the postal service would very much like to see it taxed in some manner.

## Correlative Conjunctions

Some conjunctions combine with other words to form what are called **correlative conjunctions**. They always travel in pairs, joining various sentence elements that should be treated as grammatically equal.

- She led the team not only in statistics but also by virtue of her enthusiasm.
- Polonius said, "Neither a borrower nor a lender be."
- Whether you win this race or lose it doesn't matter as long as you do your best.

Correlative conjunctions sometimes create problems in parallel form. Click **HERE** for help with those problems. Here is a brief list of common correlative conjunctions.

| | |
|---|---|
| both . . . and | neither . . . nor |
| not only . . . but also | whether . . . or |
| not . . . but | as . . . as |
| either . . . or | |

## Conjunctive Adverbs

The **conjunctive adverbs** such as *however, moreover, nevertheless, consequently, as a result* are used to create complex relationships between ideas. Refer to the section on **Coherence: Transitions Between Ideas** for an extensive list of conjunctive adverbs categorized according to their various uses and for some advice on their application within sentences (including punctuation issues).

## COMMON ERRORS WITH CONJUNCTIONS

### Error 1

(Incorrect): Though he is fat, still he runs fast.

(Correct): Though he is fat, he runs fast.

(Incorrect): As he is fast, so he can't run fast.

(Correct): As he is fast, he can't run fast. OR He is fat, so he can't run fast.

(Incorrect): As I took aim at that time he shook my arm.

(Correct): As I took aim he shook my arm.

In English, one conjunction is enough to join two clauses - we do not normally use two.

### Error 2

(Incorrect): Because he was not ready therefore we left without him.

(Correct): Because he was not ready we left without him.

The conjunction **because** is enough to join the two clauses. There is no need to use a second conjunction like **therefore** or **so**.

### Error 3

(Incorrect): She did not come to school. Because she was ill.

(Correct): She did not come to school because she was ill.

This is a common punctuation mistake. **Because** is a subordinating conjunctionand must never be separated from its main clause by a full stop.

### Error 4

(Incorrect): No sooner I had reached the station than the train left.

(Correct): No sooner had I reached the station than the train left.

When **no sooner** comes at the beginning of a sentence, we use an inverted word order. That means the auxiliary verb comes before the subject.

(Incorrect): Neither he comes nor he writes.

(Correct): Neither does he come nor does he write.

When the first word of the sentence is negative, the auxiliary verb comes before the subject. Note that the sentence *He neither comes nor writes* is equally right and probably more common.

### Error 5

(Incorrect): Their front door was open and there was nobody at home.

(Correct): Their front door was open but there was nobody at home.

**But** is the conjunction to use when the second main clause gives unexpected information.

## Chapter-8

# Determiners

A **determiner** (also called **determinative**) is a word, phrase or affix that occurs together with a noun or noun phrase and serves to express the reference of that noun or noun phrase in the context. That is, a determiner may indicate whether the noun is referring to a definite or indefinite element of a class, to a closer or more distant element, to an element belonging to a specified person or thing, to a particular number or quantity, etc. Common kinds of determiners include definite and indefinite articles (like the English *the*and *a* or *an*), demonstratives (*this* and *that*), possessive determiners (*my* and *their*), andquantifiers (*many, few* and *several*). See examples in the box on the right; and seeEnglish determiners and English articles.

### DESCRIPTION

Most determiners have been traditionally classed along with adjectives, and this still occurs: for example, demonstrative and possessive determiners are sometimes described as *demonstrative adjectives* and *possessive adjectives* respectively. However, modern theorists ofgrammar prefer to distinguish determiners as a separate word class from adjectives, which are simple modifiers of nouns, expressing attributes of the thing referred to. This distinction applies particularly in languages like English that use definite and indefinite articles, frequently as a necessary component of noun phrases – the determiners may then be taken to be a class of words that includes the articles as well as other words that function in the place of articles. (The composition of this class may depend on the particular language's rules of syntax; for example, in English the possessives *my*, *your* etc. are used without articles and so can be regarded as determiners, whereas their Italianequivalents *mio* etc. are used together with articles and so may be better classed as adjectives.) Not all languages can be said to have a lexically distinct class of determiners.

In some languages, the role of certain determiners can be played by affixes (prefixes or suffixes) attached to a noun or by other types ofinflection. For example, definite articles are represented by suffixes in Romanian, Bulgarian, Macedonian, and Swedish. (For example, in Swedish, *bok* ("book"), when definite, becomes *boken* ("the book"), while the Romanian *caiet* ("notebook") similarly becomes *caietul* ("the notebook").) Some languages, such as Finnish, have possessive affixes, which play the role of possessive determiners like *my* and *his*.

X-bar theory contends that every noun has a corresponding determiner (or specifier). In a case where a noun does not have an explicit determiner (as in *physics uses mathematics*), X-bar theory hypothesizes the presence of a zero article, or zero determiner. Noun phrases that contain only a noun and do not have a determiner present are known as bare noun phrases.

Some modern grammatical approaches regard determiners (rather than nouns) as the head of their phrase and thus refer to such phrases asdeterminer phrases rather than noun phrases. For more detail on theoretical approaches to the status of determiners, see Noun phrase: Noun phrases with and without determiners.

Some theoreticians unify determiners and pronouns into a single class. See Pronoun: Theoretical considerations.

Universal Grammar is the theory that all humans are born equipped with grammar, and all languages share certain properties. There are arguments that determiners are not a part of Universal Grammar and are instead part of an emergent syntactic category. This has been shown through the studies of some languages' histories, including Dutch.

## Types of determiners

- Articles
- Demonstratives
- Possessives
- Quantifiers
- Numerals
- Distributives
- Interrogatives

For details of the use of determiners in English, see English determiners (and specifically for the definite and indefinite articles, English articles).

## Determiners

Determiners are a kind of noun modifier; they precede and are necessarily followed by nouns. While adjectives perform a similar function, the term 'determiner' refers to a relatively limited set of well-established words that can be said to 'mark' nouns.

The function of determiners is to 'express reference'; i. e. they clarify what a noun is referring to. For example when one says 'that box', the listener knows which box is being referred to.

There are many types of determiners:

### 1. *Articles*

There are three articles: a, an, and the.

*Indefinite Articles*

A and an are indefinite articles that serve the same purpose, but they cannot be used interchangeably, because 'a' is only used before words that begin with consonants, and 'an' is used only before words that begin with vowels. (Note: 'an' before 'h' when it is silent, as in 'hour' and 'honour'; 'a' before 'u' and 'eu' when they sound like 'you', as in 'European' and 'university'.

The uses of the indefinite article are as follows:

1. To refer to some member of a group, class or category. For example He is a doctor (profession)/an Indian (nationality)/a Hindu (religion).
2. To refer to a kind of, or example of something. For example He has a large nose/a thick beard/a strange aunt.
3. Preceding singular nouns, with the words 'what' and 'such'. For example What a car! Oh, that's such a shame!
4. To mean 'one' object, whether a person or thing. For example The thieves stole a necklace and a portrait.
5. To refer to something that is being mentioned for the first time. For example There was a chill in the air.

   Note:

1. We usually say a hundred, a thousand, a million, etc.
2. 'A' is not indiscriminately used to refer to singular objects; 'one' is used when emphasis is required. For example There is only one way out of this mess.

### *Definite Article*

'The' is known as the definite article in English. Its uses are as follows:

1. When something is being referred to that has already been mentioned. For example I saw a pretty girl at the mall today. The pretty girl did not, however, see me.
2. When both parties involved in the conversation are aware of what is being discussed. For example Where is the restroom?
3. To refer to unique objects. For example the sun, the moon, the Earth, the Taj Mahal.
4. With superlatives and ordinal numbers (numbers used to rank a set of objects). For example Mt Everest is the tallest mountain on earth, Neil Armstrong was the first man on the moon.
5. To refer to groups of people, geographical areas and oceans, and with decades or groups of years. For example the Americans, the Sahara/Pacific, the fifties/sixities/seventies/eighties.

## 2. *Quantifiers*

See article on Quantifiers.

## 3. *Demonstratives*

This, that, these and those are known are demonstratives; they describe the position of an object, seen from the speaker's viewpoint.

This and these (used for singular and plural nouns respectively) refer to objects that close by. For example Whose car is this? Whose cars are these?

That and those (used for singular and plural nouns respectively) refer to objects that are further away. The closeness can be physical or psychological. For example Who lives in that house?

## 4. *Numbers*

Numbers are cardinal (one, two, three, etc) and ordinal (first, second, third, etc). Cardinal numbers are adjectives that indicate quantity (There are fives apples on the table), and ordinal numbers indicate rank or order (This is the first time for me on a plane).

## 5. *Distributives*

The words all, both, half, each, every, either and neither are known as distributives.

All, Both, Half

These three words can be used in the following ways:

**All +** uncountable noun

Don Bradman is the greatest batsman of all time.

'the' + uncountable noun/countable noun in plural form

We have all the time in the world.

All the people in the hall went quiet.

'my', 'your', etc + uncountable noun/countable noun in plural form

All my life I have been waiting for this moment.

All you friends have been invited to the party.

'this', 'that' + uncountable noun/'these', 'those' + countable noun in plural form

Look at all this dust!

I do not have time for all these formalities.

**Both +**

'the' /'my', 'your', etc/'these', 'those' + countable noun in plural form (note: used only when two objects are being referred to)

Both the dogs have passed away.

Both my ankles have been hurting since I jumped from the balcony.

Both these books must be returned within the week.

**Half +**

'a' + uncountable noun

We bought half a kilo of rice.

'the'/'my', 'your', etc/'this', 'that', 'these', 'those' + noun

Half the village perished in the floods.

I spent half my inheritance on travelling the world.

You may have half (of) this cake.

Only half (of) those points are relevant.

Each, Every, Either, Neither

See articles.

### *6. Possessives*

Possessive pronouns and adjectives indicate who an object belongs to.

The pronouns are

mine (first person: This car is mine = I own this car)

yours (second person: This car is yours = You own this car)

his, hers, and its (third person: This cars is his/hers = He/she owns this car).

The corresponding adjectives are

my

your
his, her, and it

*7. Difference words*

Other and another are 'difference words'; they refer to something different, or remaining, or more. Other is used with singular and plural nouns, while another is used strictly with singular nouns.

What other colours can I get this in?

Is there another colour that this is available in?

*8. Defining words*

Which and whose are 'defining words'; they indicate which thing or person is being referred to.

This is the house which I used to live in as a child.

This is the man whose window you broke.

## ENGLISH DETERMINERS

An important role in English grammar is played by determiners – words or phrases that precede a noun or noun phrase and serve to express its reference in the context. The most common of these are the definite and indefinite articles, *the* and *a(n)*. Other determiners in English include demonstratives such as *this* and *that*, possessives such as *my* and *the boy's*, and quantifiers such as *all*, *many* and *three*.

In many contexts the presence of some determiner is required in order to form a complete noun phrase. However, in some cases complete noun phrases are formed without any determiner (sometimes referred to as "zero determiner" or "zero article"), as in the sentence *Apples are fruit*. Determiners can also be used in certain combinations, as in *my many friends* or *all the chairs*.

### Overview

The terminology used in accounts of English grammar to refer to determiners is very varied. Sometimes the term is not used at all, and the words classed here as determiners (apart from the articles) are classed as adjectives (but see Determiners and adjectives below). In the present article a broad view is taken of what constitutes a determiner; it includes the articles and words and phrases that can substitute for them, as well as words and phrases serving as quantifiers. This means that determiners as construed here include words from the determiner class, such as *the, this, my, many,* etc., as well as nominal possessives (*John's, the tall boy's*) and other specifying or quantifying phrases such as *more than three, almost all,* and *this size* (as in *this size shoes*).

Note that many words or phrases that serve as determiners can also play the role of pronouns; for example, the word *all* is a determiner in the sentences *All men are equal* and *I know all the rules,* but a pronoun in *All's well that ends well.* In other cases there is a related but distinct pronoun form; for example the determiners *my* and *no* have corresponding pronouns *mine* and *none.*

Determiners that consist of phrases rather than single words might be called *determiner phrases,* although this should probably be avoided as the term is also used to refer to a noun phrase headed by a determiner. An alternative term is *phrasal determiners.*

## Common determiners

The following is a rough classification of determiners used in English, including both words and phrases:

- *Definite determiners,* which imply that the referent of the resulting noun phrase is defined specifically:
- The definite article *the.*
- The demonstratives *this* and *that,* with respective plural forms *these* and *those.*
- Possessives, including those corresponding to pronouns – *my, your, his, her, its, our, their, whose* – and the Saxon genitives formed from other nouns, pronouns and noun phrases (*one's, everybody's, Mary's, a boy's, the man we saw yesterday's*). These can be made more emphatic with the addition of *own* or *very own.*

- Interrogatives *which, what* (these can be followed by *-ever* for emphasis).
- Relative determiners: *which* (quite formal and archaic, as in *He acquired two dogs and three cats, which animals were then...)*; also*whichever* and *whatever* (which are of the type that form clauses with no antecedent: *I'll take whatever money they've got*).

*Indefinite determiners*:

- The indefinite article *a* or *an* (the latter is used when followed by a vowel sound).
- The word *some*, pronounced [s(Y)m], used as an equivalent of the indefinite article with plural and non-count nouns (a partitive).
- The strong form of *some*, pronounced [sŒm], as in *Some people prefer dry wine*; this can also be used with singular count nouns (*There's some man at the door*). For words such as *certain* and *other* see below.
- The word *any*, often used in negative and interrogative contexts in place of the article-equivalent *some* (and sometimes also with singular count nouns). It can also be used to express alternative.

*Quantifiers*, which quantify a noun:

- Basic words indicating a large or small quantity: *much/many, little/few*, and their comparative and superlative forms *more, most, less/fewer, least/fewest*. Where two forms are given, the first is used with non-count nouns and the second with count nouns (although in colloquial English *less* and *least* are frequently also used with count nouns). The basic forms can be modified with adverbs, especially *very, too* and *so* (and *not* can also be added). Note that unmodified *much* is quite rarely used in affirmative statements in colloquial English.
- Phrases expressing similar meanings to the above: *a lot of, lots of, plenty of, a great deal of, tons of*, etc. Many such phrases can alternatively be analyzed as nouns followed by a preposition, but their treatment as phrasal determiners is supported by the fact that the resulting noun phrase takes

the number of the following noun, not the noun in the phrase (*a lot of people* would take a plural verb, even though *lot* is singular).

- Words and phrases expressing some unspecified or probably quite small amount: *a few/a little* (learners often confuse these with*few/little*), *several, a couple of, a bit of, a number of* etc.
- Cardinal numbers: *zero* (quite rare as determiner), *one, two,* etc. In some analyses these may not be treated as determiners.
- Other phrases expressing precise quantity: *a pair of, five litres of,* etc.
- Words and phrases expressing multiples or fractions: *half, half of, double, twice, three times, twice as much,* etc. Those like *double*and *half* (without *of*) are generally used in combination with definite determiners.
- Words expressing maximum, sufficient or zero quantity: *all, both, enough, sufficient, no.*
- Note that many of these quantifiers can be modified by adverbs and adverbial phrases such as *almost, over, more than, less than,* when the meaning is appropriate.

Words that enumerate over a group or class, or indicate alternatives:

- *each, every* (note that *every* can be modified by adverbs such as *almost* and *practically,* whereas *each* generally cannot. However, also note *every other,* which refers to each second member in a series.)
- *any* (as in *any dream will do;* see also under *indefinite determiners* above), *either, neither*

*Personal determiners*:

- The words *you* and *we/us,* in phrases like *we teachers; you guys* can be analysed as determiners.

Examples:

"As all we teachers know..."

"Us girls must stick together. "(informal)

These examples can be contrasted with a similar but different use of *pronouns* in an appositional construction, where the use of other pronouns is also permitted but the pronouns *cannot* be preceded by the (pre-) determiner "all".

Examples:

"I/we, the undersigned,..., "

"We, the undersigned,..., "

but *not*

- All we, the undersigned,..."

Other cases:

- The words *such* and exclamative *what* (these are followed by an indefinite article when used with a singular noun, as in *such a treat, what a disaster!*)
- Noun phrases used as determiners, such as *this colour, what size* and *how many* (as in *I like this colour furniture; What size shoes do you take?; How many candles are there?)*
- Words such as *same, other, certain, different, only*, which serve a determining function, but are grammatically more likely to be classed simply as adjectives, in that they generally require another determiner to complete the phrase (although they still come before other adjectives). Note that the indefinite article in combination with *other* is written as the single word *another*.

Consult Wiktionary for more information on the meanings and usage of the words listed here. It also contains a fairly complete list of words that can be classed as determiners in English.

## ZERO DETERMINER

In some contexts a complete noun phrase can exist without any determiner (or with "zero determiner"). The main types of such cases are:

- with plural or uncountable nouns used to refer to a concept or members of a class generally: *cars are useful* (but *the cars* when specific cars are being referred to); *happiness is contagious* (but *the happiness* when specific happiness is referred to, as in *the happiness that laughter engenders...).*
- with plural or uncountable nouns used to refer to some unspecified amount of something: *there are cats in the kitchen;*

*I noticed water on the floor* (here it is also possible to use *some cats, some water*).

- with many proper names: *Tom Smith, Birmingham, Italy, Jupiter.*
- with singular common nouns in some common expressions: *smiling from ear to ear, leaving town today.*

For more information, see English articles.

Combinations of determiners

Determiners can be used in certain combinations. Common examples are listed below:

- A definite determiner can be followed by certain quantifiers (*the many problems, these three things, my very few faults*).
- The words *all* and *both* can be followed by a definite determiner (*all the green apples, both the boys*), which can also be followed by a quantifier as above (*all the many outstanding issues*).
- The word *all* can be followed by a cardinal number (*all three things*).
- The word *some* can be followed by a cardinal number (*some eight packets*, meaning "approximately eight").
- Words and phrases expressing fractions and multiples, such as *half, double, twice, three times*, etc. can be followed by a definite determiner (*half a minute, double the risk, twice my age, three times my salary, three-quarters the diameter*, etc.
- The words *such* and exclamative *what* can be followed by an indefinite article (as mentioned in the section above).
- The word *many* can be used with the indefinite article and a singular noun (*many a night, many an awkward moment*).
- The words *each* and *every* can be followed by a cardinal number or other expression of definite quantity (*each two seats, every five grams of flour*).

To specify a quantity within a definite class (as opposed to a definite class of a given quantity), it is often possible to use a quantifier in pronoun form (often identical to the determiner form), followed by *of* and a definite determiner. For example, *three of the mice, few of my enemies, none of these pictures, much of John's information.* An alternative construction with possessives is to place *of* and the pronoun form of the possessive after the noun: *few enemies of mine, much information of John's.*

As with other parts of speech, it is often possible to connect determiners of the same type with the conjunctions *and* and *or*: *his and her children, two or three beans*.

## Determiners and adjectives

In traditional English grammar, determiners were not considered a separate part of speech – most of them would have been classed asadjectives. However there are certain differences between determiners and ordinary adjectives (although the boundary is not always entirely clear).

- Determiners take the place (or can take the place) of articles in noun phrases, whereas adjectives do not. For example, *my house* (not **the my house*), but *the big house*.
- Adjectives can generally be used in combination without restriction, whereas only certain combinations of determiners are allowable. For example, *a big green book* is grammatical, but **every his book* is not.
- Most adjectives can be used alone in predicative complement position, as in *he is happy*; determiners cannot (**he is the* is not a grammatical sentence), except where the same words are used as pronouns (*the problem is this*).
- Most adjectives have comparative and superlative forms (*happier, happiest; more beautiful, most beautiful*), whereas determiners generally are not (except *much/many, few, little*).
- Determiners often have corresponding pronouns, while adjectives do not.
- Adjectives can modify singular or plural nouns, while determiners are sometimes restricted to one or the other (as with *much* and *many*).

When determiners and adjectives (or other modifiers) occur in the same noun phrase, the determiner generally comes first: *the big book*, not **big the book*. However there are certain exceptions when the determiner is the indefinite article *a(n)*: that article normally comes after an adjective modified with *so, as, too* or *how*. For example:

- *It was so terrible a disease that...* (alternatively:... *such a terrible disease that...)*

- *He was as rude a man as I have ever met.*
- *That was too good an opportunity to miss.*
- *I know how good a swimmer she is.*

For more information about theoretical approaches to the status of determiners, see Noun phrase: Noun phrases with and without determiners.

## COMMON ERRORS ON DETERMINER (A, AN, THE, MANY, MUCH, A, FEW, ETC)

### Common errors

1. wrong: he eats apple one day
   Right: He eats an apple a day
2. wrong-Dog got tail
   Right- A dog has a tail
3. Wrong-He phoned taxi. Where's taxi?
   Right-He phoned for a taxi. Where's the taxi?
4. Wrong- I have much money, but not much coins.
   Right-I have a lot of money, but not many coins.
5. Wrong-Road is clear. There no traffic.
   Right- The road is clear. There isn't any traffic.

### Notes on correct usage

1. Use 'a' before a consonant sound. (He's a student)
2. Use 'an' before a vowel sound. (I sent an e mail)
3. Also use 'an' before a silent 'h' (He will be her by an hour)
4. Use 'the' when referring to a particular thing. (That's the car. That's the stolen car)
5. Use these expressions with uncountable nouns: (Not much rain, a great deal of rain, a littlewater, a lot of snow, plenty of dust)
6. For countable nouns, use these expressions. (A few cars, many houses, a lot of people, anyboxes in there? Several boxes, plenty of seats)

## Chapter-9

# Idioms and Interjections

### IDIOM

An idiom is a phrase or a fixed expression that has a figurative, or sometimes literal, meaning. An idiom's figurative meaning is different from the literalmeaning. There are thousands of idioms, and they occur frequently in all languages. It is estimated that there are at least twenty-five thousand idiomatic expressions in the English language.

#### Examples

The following sentences contain idioms. The fixed words constituting the idiom in each case are bolded:

a. She is **pulling** my **leg**. - *to pull someone's leg* means to trick them by telling them something untrue.
b. When will you **drop** them **a line**? - *to drop someone a line* means to send a note to or call someone.
c. You should **keep an eye out for** that. - *to keep an eye out for something* means to maintain awareness of it so that you notice it as it occurs.
d. I can't **keep** my **head above water**. - *to keep one's head above water* means to manage a situation.
e. It's **raining cats and dogs**. - *to rain cats and dogs* means to rain very heavily (a downpour).
f. Oh no! You **spilled the beans!** - *to spill the beans* means to let out a secret.

g. Why are you **feeling blue**? - *to feel blue* means to feel sad.

h. That jacket costs **an arm and a leg**. – *an arm and a leg* means something is very expensive.

i. It is **not rocket science**. – *not rocket science* means something is *not difficult*.

j. Put a **cork in it**. - *put a cork in it* is an impolite way to say, "shut up!" (another idiom), be quiet, and stop talking.

k. I'm **screwed**. - *to be screwed* means that one is doomed, is in big trouble, or has really messed up.

Each of the word combinations in bold has at least two meanings: a literal meaning and a figurative meaning. Such expressions that are typical for a language can appear as words, combinations of words, phrases, entire clauses, and entire sentences.

l. **The devil is in the details.**

m. **The early bird gets the worm.**

n. **Break a leg.**

o. **Waste not, want not.**

p. **Go take a chill pill.**

q. **I have butterflies in my stomach.**

Expressions such as these have figurative meaning. When one says "The devil is in the details", one is not expressing a belief in demons, but rather one means that things may look good on the surface, but upon scrutiny, undesirable aspects are revealed. Similarly, when one says "The early bird gets the worm", one is not suggesting that there is only one worm, rather one means there are plenty of worms, but for the sake of the idiom one plays along, and imagines that there is only one worm. On the other hand, "Waste not, want not" is completely devoid of a figurative meaning. It counts as an idiom, however, because it has a literal meaning and people keep saying it.

## Derivations

Many idiomatic expressions, in their original use were not figurative but had literal meaning.

For instance: *spill the beans* meaning to let out a secret probably originates in a physical spilling of beans which are either being eaten or measured out. The point is that the spiller certainly does not want to lose any beans. Or, alternatively, it may be that a person wants to share a secret, and finally, perhaps after prodding, does so, and when that happens it would be like spilling beans into a bowl or other appropriate container.

*let the cat out of the bag* : has a meaning similar to the former, but the secret revealed in this case will likely cause some problems. A cat was sometimes put in a bag to keep it under control or to pretend that it was a more saleable animal, such as a pig or a rabbit. So, to let the cat out of the bag suggests either that the ruse is revealed or that the situation is out of control. Or alternatively, it may be that the way a cat, once set free, will wander off was a good description of a secret that is revealed.

*break a leg*: meaning good luck in a performance/ presentation etc. This common idiom comes from belief in superstitions. The term 'break a leg' appears to come from the belief that one ought not to utter the words 'good luck' to an actor. By wishing someone bad luck, it is supposed that the opposite will occur.

## Compositionality

In linguistics, idioms are usually presumed to be figures of speech contradicting the principle of compositionality. This principle states that the meaning of a whole should be constructed from the meanings of the parts that make up the whole. In other words, one should be in a position to understand the whole if one understands the meanings of each of the parts that make up the whole. The following example is widely employed to illustrate the point:

**Fred kicked the bucket.**

Understood compositionally, Fred has literally kicked an actual, physical bucket. The much more likely idiomatic reading, however, is non-compositional: Fred is understood to have died. Arriving at the idiomatic reading from the literal reading is unlikely for most speakers. What this means is that the idiomatic reading is, rather, stored as a single lexical item that is now largely independent of the literal reading.

In phraseology, idioms are defined as a sub-type of phraseme, the meaning of which is not the regular sum of the meanings of its component parts. John Saeed defines an idiom as collocated words that became affixed to each other until metamorphosing into a fossilised term. This collocation of words redefines each component word in the word-group and becomes an *idiomatic expression*. Idioms usually do not translate well; in some cases, when an idiom is translated directly word-for-word into another language, either its meaning is changed or it is meaningless.

When two or three words are often used together in a particular sequence, the words are said to be irreversible binomials, or Siamese twins. Usage will prevent the words from being displaced or rearranged. For example, a person may be left "high and dry" but never "dry and high". This idiom in turn means that the person is left in their former condition rather than being assisted so that their condition improves. Not all Siamese twins are idioms, however. "Chips and dip" is an irreversible binomial, but it refers to literal food items, not idiomatic ones.

## TRANSLATING IDIOMS

Literal translation (word-by-word) of opaque idioms will not convey the same meaning in other languages. Idioms from other languages that are analogous to *kick the bucket* in English are listed next:

**Arabic**: Wad'aa" he said goodbye

**Afrikaans**: *lepel deur die dak steek* 'to push a spoon through the ceiling (roof)',

**Bulgarian**: *ăà ðèòíåø êàìáàíàòà* 'to kick the bell'

**Czech**: *natáhnout baèkory* 'pull the slippers'

**Danish**: *at stille træskoene* 'to take off the clogs',

**Dutch**: *het loodje leggen* 'to lay the piece of lead' or *de pijp aan Maarten geven* 'to give the pipe to Maarten',

**Farsi**: *daare faani raa vedaa' goft* 'said goodbye to the mortal dwelling',

**Filipino**: *magbalat-kayo* 'to pretend to be someone he's not' or 'to hide one's true identity'

**Finnish**: *potkaista tyhjää* 'to kick the void' or *heittää veivinsä* 'to toss away the crank' or *kasvaa koiranputkea* 'to be growing cow parsley' or *heittää lusikan nurkkaan* 'to toss the spoon to the corner' or *oikaista koipensa* 'to stretch the shanks'

**French**: *manger des pissenlits par la racine* 'to eat dandelions by the root' or *casser sa pipe* 'to break his pipe' or *passer l'arme à gauche* 'pass the weapon to the left',

**German**: *den Löffel abgeben* 'to give the spoon away' or *ins Gras beißen* 'to bite into the grass' or *sich die Radieschen von unten ansehen* 'look at the radishes from underneath',

**Hindi**: *Patta kat jana* 'to cut the leaf'

**Hungarian**: *Feldobja a lábát* 'to throw his foot up' or *Fûbe harap* 'to bite into the grass' or *Alulról szagolja az ibolyát* 'to smell the viola from underneath' or *Elpatkolt* 'to fail shoeing (a horse)',

**Greek**: *ôéíÜæù ôá ðÝôáëá* 'to shake the horse-shoes',

**Icelandic**: *Að geispa golunni* 'to yawn the breeze',

**Italian**: *tirare le cuoia* 'to pull the skins',

**Latvian**: *nolikt karoti* 'to put the spoon down'

**Lithuanian**: *pakratyti kojas* 'to shake the legs',

**Norwegian**: *å parkere tøflene* 'to park the slippers',

**Polish**: *kopn[1]æ w kalendarz* 'to kick the calendar', *wyci[1]gn[1]æ kopyta* 'to stretch the hooves', *w[1]chaæ kwiatki od spodu* 'to smell the flowers from underneath', 'wsi[1]œæ w czarny autobus' 'to get on a black bus', 'pójœæ na tamten œwiat' 'go to the other world', 'waln[1]æ w ramy' 'to hit the frame',

**Portuguese**: *bater as botas* 'to beat the boots', *esticar o pernil* 'to stretch the leg', or *fazer tijolo* 'to make a brick', plus *comer capim pela raiz* 'to eat grass by the root', *abotoar o paletó* 'to button up the blazer/coat', *esticar as canelas* 'to stretch the shanks',

**Romanian**: *a da colul* 'to turn the corner', or *i-a sunat ceasul* 'his clock has rung',

**Russian**: *ñûãðàòü â ÿùèê* (sygrat' v yaschik) 'to play into the box', *äàòü äóáà* 'to give the oak', *îòêèíóòü êîïûòà* 'to throw back the hoofs'

**Slovenian**: *šel je rakom žvižgat* 'he went to whistle to the crabs',

**Spanish**: *estirar la pata* 'to stretch the leg' or *palmarla* 'to pop off'

**Swedish**: *trilla av pinnen* 'to roll off the stick' very similar to 'walk the plank'. (as in a parrot or other bird suddenly dying and falling off its perch), *ta ner skylten* 'take the sign down' or *sätta skorna* 'take the shoes off'

**Tlingit**: *dákde kákw aawayaa* 'to take one's basket into the woods',

**Turkish**: *Nallarý dikti' 'put the horseshoes in the air', as in a horse dropped dead to the ground,*

**Ukrainian**: *âð³çàòè äóáà* 'to cut the oak (as in building a coffin)',

**Urdu**: *Haathi nikal gaya dum phans gaya ÀÇÊªÌ ä˜á ÌÇ Ïã ªäÓ ÆÌ* 'The elephant escaped but his tail got stuck'

Some idioms are transparent. Much of their meaning does get through if they are taken (or translated) literally. For example, *lay one's cards on the table* meaning to reveal previously unknown intentions, or to reveal a secret. Transparency is a matter of degree; *spill the beans* (to let secret information become known) and *leave no stone unturned* (to do everything possible in order to achieve or find something) are not entirely literally interpretable, but only involve a slight metaphorical broadening. Another category of idioms is a word having several meanings, sometimes simultaneously, sometimes discerned from the context of its usage. This is seen in the (mostly uninflected) English language in polysemes, the common use of the same word for an activity, for those engaged in it, for the product used, for the place or time of an activity, and sometimes for a verb.

Idioms tend to confuse those unfamiliar with them; students of a new language must learn its idiomatic expressions as vocabulary. Manynatural language words have *idiomatic origins*, but are assimilated, so losing their figurative senses, for example, in Portuguese, the expression *saber de coração* 'to know by heart', with the same meaning as in English, was shortened to 'saber de cor', and, later, to the verb*decorar*, meaning *memorize*.

## Dealing with non-compositionality

The non-compositionality of meaning of idioms challenges theories of syntax. The fixed words of many idioms do not qualify as constituents in any sense, e. g.

a. How do we **get to the bottom of** this situation?

The fixed words of this idiom (in bold) do not form a constituent in any theory's analysis of syntactic structure because the object of the preposition (here *this situation*) is not part of the idiom (but rather it is an argument of the idiom). One can know that it is not part of the idiom because it is variable, e. g. *How do we get to the bottom of this situation / the claim / the phenomenon / her statement* / etc. What this means is that theories of syntax that take the constituent to be the fundamental unit of syntactic analysis are challenged. The manner in which units of meaning are assigned to units of syntax remains unclear. This problem has motivated a tremendous amount of discussion and debate in linguistics circles and it is a primary motivator behind the Construction Grammar framework.

## Interjections

In grammar, an **interjection** or **exclamation** may be a word used to express an emotion or sentiment on the part of the speaker (although most interjections have clear definitions). Filled pauses such as *uh, er, um* are also considered interjections. Interjections are often placed at the beginning of a sentence.

An interjection is sometimes expressed as a single word or non-sentence phrase, followed by a punctuation mark. The isolated usage of an interjection does not represent a complete sentence in conventional English writing. Thus, in formal writing, the interjection will be incorporated into a larger sentence clause. Interjection as a figure of speech refers to the use of one word. For example, lawyers in the United States of America traditionally say: *Objection!* or soldiers: *Fire!*.

## Examples in English

Conventions like *Hi, Bye* and *Goodbye* are interjections, as are exclamations like *Cheers!* and *Hooray!*. In fact, like a noun or a pronoun, they are very often characterized by exclamation marks depending on the stress of the attitude or the force of the emotion they are expressing. *Well* (a short form of "that is well") can also be used as an interjection: "Well! That's great!" or "Well, don't worry." Much profanity takes the form of interjections. Some linguists consider the pro-sentences *yes, no, amen* and *okay* as interjections, since they have no syntactical connection with other words and rather work as sentences themselves. Expressions such as "Excuse me!", "Sorry!", "No thank you!", "Oh dear!", "Hey that's mine!", and similar ones often serve as interjections. Interjections can be phrases or even sentences, as well as words, such as "Oh!" "Pooh!" "Wow!" or "sup!".

## Phonology

Several English interjections contain sounds, or are sounds as opposed to words, that do not (or very rarely) exist in regular Englishphonological inventory. For example:

- *Ahem* [Y"Ym], ["Y"Ym], [YfYm], or ["YhYm], ("attention!") may contain a glottal stop ["] or a [f] in any dialect of English; the glottal stop is common in American English, some British dialects, and in other languages, such as German.
- *Gah* [aæh] ("Gah, there's nothing to do!") ends with [h], which does not occur with regular English words.
- *Oops*, an interjection made in response to the observation of a minor mistake, usually written as "Oops!" or "Whoops!"
- *Psst* [psÐ] ("here!"), is another entirely consonantal syllable-word, and its consonant cluster does not occur initially in regular English words.
- *Shh* [*f*ÐÐ] ("quiet!") is an entirely consonantal syllable.
- *Tut-tut* [À À] ("shame..."), also spelled *tsk-tsk,* is made up entirely of clicks, which are an active part of regular speech in several Africanlanguages. This particular click is dental. (This also has the spelling pronunciation [tŒt tŒt].)

- *Ugh* [Œx] ("disgusting!") ends with a velar fricative consonant, which is otherwise restricted to just a few regional dialects of English, though is common in languages like Spanish, German, Gaelic and Russian.
- *Whew* or *phew* [xju] ("what a relief!"), also spelled *shew*, may start with a bilabial fricative, a sound pronounced with a strong puff of air through the lips. This sound is a common phoneme in such languages as Suki (a language of New Guinea) and Ewe and Logba (both spoken in Ghana).
- *Yeah* [j[] ("yes") ends with the short vowel [[], or in some dialects [æ], neither of which are found at the end of any regular English words.

## Interjections

An interjection is a word that expresses some kind of emotion. It can be used as filler. Interjections do not have a grammatical function in the sentence and are not related to the other parts of the sentence. If an interjection is omitted, the sentence still makes sense. It can stand alone.

- Ouch! That hurts.
- Well, I need a break.
- Wow! What a beautiful dress!

When you are expressing a strong emotion, use an exclamation mark (!). A comma (,) can be used for a weaker emotion.

Interjections do the following:

1. Express a feeling—wow, gee, oops, darn, geez, oh:
   - Oops, I'm sorry. That was my mistake.
   - Geez! Do I need to do it again?
   - Oh, I didn't know that.
2. Say yes or no—yes, no, nope:
   - Yes! I will do it!
   - No, I am not going to go there.
   - Nope. That's not what I want.
3. Call attention—yo, hey:
   - Yo, will you throw the ball back?

- Hey, I just wanted to talk to you about the previous incident.

4. Indicate a pause—well, um, hmm:
   - Well, what I meant was nothing like that.
   - Um, here is our proposal.
   - Hmm. You really need to be on a diet.

## Interjections

**Interjections** are words or phrases used to exclaim or protest or command. They sometimes stand by themselves, but they are often contained within larger structures.

- Wow! I won the lottery!
- Oh, I don't know about that.
- I don't know what the heck you're talking about.
- No, you shouldn't have done that.

Most mild interjections are treated as **parenthetical elements** and set off from the rest of the sentence with a comma or set of commas. If the interjection is more forceful, however, it is followed with an **exclamation mark**. Interjections are rarely used in formal or academic writing.

## What Is An Interjection?

An interjection is one of the eight major parts of speech along with verbs, nouns, pronouns, adjectives, adverbs, prepositions and conjunctions. Some grammarians believe that interjections are the least important part of speech. This is because interjections are not generally required in order for the meaning of a sentence to become clear.

An interjection is a word solely designed to convey emotion. It expresses meaning or feeling. It does not:

- relate grammatically to the other parts of the sentence
- help the reader understand the relationship between words and phrases in the sentence

Instead, it simply conveys to the reader the way the author is feeling. Interjections are rarely used in academic or formal writing, but are common in fiction or artistic writing. They are usually, but not always, offset by an exclamation point (which is also used to show emotion).

## USE OF INTERJECTIONS

### Beginning of Sentences

When people think of interjections, they commonly think of them being used at the beginning of the sentence. Many also associate interjections with a punctuation mark designed to convey emotion: the exclamation point.

This is often true. Interjections can and do appear in the beginning of sentences. For example:

- "Yikes, I didn't realize that there was a test on grammar today!"
- "Oh no, I can't believe that it is snowing here again!"

In both of these sentences the interjection - "yikes" and "oh no" appear at the beginning of the sentence. In addition, in both of the sentences, the emotion is a strong emotion and the sentence itself ends with an exclamation point.

### Middle or End of Sentences

Interjections do not always have to be at the beginning of a sentence. They can appear in the middle, at the end, or anyplace else where the author wants to interject a bit of feeling and emotion.

For example, in the sentence "So, it's snowing again, huh?" the interjection is found at the end. Here, the interjection is designed to express confusion (or perhaps dismay) at the continued snow falling. In this sentence, the emotion wasn't an emotion that necessitated an exclamation point—instead, the interjection 'huh' turned the sentence into a question.

The sentence "In my opinion, my gosh, this is just the smartest thing you have ever said" the interjection is found in the middle. It designed to express or convey the author's emphasis on his opinion that the statement was smart. Again, no exclamation point is required.

## Stand-alone Sentence

An interjection can also be used by itself as a stand-alone sentence. For example, look at the two sentences: "Oh gosh! I can't believe how late it is." The interjection "oh gosh" is a stand-alone sentence. This is grammatically correct, although "Oh Gosh" does not contain a subject and action that is normally required for a complete thought to be expressed. The interjection—or the emotion felt—is the entire point of the sentence.

## Types of Interjections

There are literally hundreds, if not thousands, of interjections in the English language. Most are designed to express strong emotions, such as love, hate, surprise, happiness, anger, enthusiasm, disgust, boredom, confusion or unhappiness. However, this is not always true. Some interjections can express either a mild emotion, or can be expressions, such as "Excuse me."

A sample list of interjections includes words such as:

- Aha
- Boo
- Crud
- Dang
- Eew
- Gosh
- Goodness
- Ha
- Oh
- Oops
- Oh no
- Ouch
- Rats
- Shoot
- Uh-oh
- Uh-huh

- Ugh
- Yikes
- Yuck

This is by no means an exhaustive list, but is representative of the types of interjections you may use on a daily basis. For more examples see Examples of Interjections.

## Identifying Interjections

Now that you've looked at a list of interjections, practice identifying them in these ten sentences:

1. Yowza! That is a fine looking car.
2. Hurray! It is a snow day and school is cancelled.
3. It is so exciting, my goodness, I just can't believe it.
4. Joe was late to school and yikes, the teacher was mad.
5. Oh! I can't believe how nice you look.
6. Well, gee, that sure is a kind thing to say.
7. Boo! I scared you.
8. Woops, I dropped the milk and it spilled.
9. Yay, it is finally Friday and the work week is over.
10. Oh well, all good things must come to an end.

Answers to Identifying Interjections:

1. Yowza! That is a fine looking car: Yowza is the interjection here. It is expressing the emotion of being quite impressed with the car.
2. Hurray! It is a snow day and school is cancelled Hurray is the emotion here. Clearly, it is expressing happiness.
3. It is so exciting, my goodness, I just can't believe it. My goodness is the interjection here, expressing excitement.
4. Joe was late to school and yikes, the teacher was mad. Yikes is the emotion being expressed here.
5. Oh! I can't believe how nice you look. Oh, the interjection, acts as a classic interjection at the beginning of a sentence. It is offset by its exclamation point.
6. Well, gee, that sure is a kind thing to say. Here, we have two interjections: well and gee.

7. Boo! I scared you. Boo is the rather obvious (and scary) interjection in this sentence.
8. Woops, I dropped the milk and it spilled. Woops is the interjection used to express the error.
9. Yay, it is finally Friday and the work week is over. Yay is another interjection that expresses the emotion of happiness, just as hurray did in sentence #2.
10. Oh well, all good things must come to an end. Oh well is the emotion here, an interjection with a tinge of resignation.

## Interjections in Writing

Interjections are not commonly used in formal or academic writing. Because of the function that interjections serve, there is virtually no place for them in an academic paper that is designed to convey facts. By definition, facts should be devoid of emotion or opinion such as the emotions conveyed by interjections.

Interjections are used most often in speech. While people don't necessarily pause to think about it, they use interjections all the time. This is even more true when you consider the fact that common words used in pauses, such as "uh," and "um" are interjections.

Interjections can find their way into fictional pieces, most often in the form of dialogue. They can also be used in informal written communication between two people, such as letters or emails.

## Uses of Interjections

Interjections are used to communicate an extreme emotion which is difficult to verbalize, or to get someone's attention. They're usually found at the beginning of the sentence. Because they are not grammatically connected to the rest of the sentence, they are often followed by an exclamation mark (or sometimes a comma).

Gee, I love old movies!

Whoa! That's a lot of homework!

Oh, drat! It seems we forgot to pay the electrical bill.

Sometimes, we use a word which usually has meaning, but in the context of the sentence it's merely for emphasis.

What was I talking about? Oh, yes, now I remember....

Here, *yes* is not actually being use as an affirmation (to answer "yes" to a question). It's just an interjection.

We thought Max wasn't coming to the family reunion and then, good lord, there he was!

*Good lord* isn't being used to address any god; it's just adding emphasis to the fact that Max had unexpectedly arrived at the family reunion.

What Are Interjections?

Interjections are words like *wow* and *yay*. They're sounds we make – to convey extreme emotion or to create emphasis – when we're talking, sometimes when we can't think of a good way to express ourselves. The problem with interjections is that, because they're technically meaningless, they require a great deal of context to be understood. For instance, *hey* can mean *hello*, or *that's great*, or *stop doing that*.

Hey! How are you?

Hey! That's an awesome hat!

Hey! Cut that out!

Interjections are frequently followed by an exclamation mark.

Interjections (and exclamation marks) are generally frowned upon in formal writing.

Interjections are not grammatically connected to any part of the sentence (i. e. they don't modify a verb or a noun, etc.) They can be removed without creating confusion.

## Interjections

This sentence is linguistically incomprehensible (i. e. we can't understand what is being discussed), but we understand the tone it implies: the speaker is clearly worked up about something. We don't know whether the speaker is happy or angry, but if we heard this sentence while walking down the street, we'd all turn our heads and look to see what exciting thing is happening.

Incomprehensible sounds such as "Whoa!" are used in the above sentence – or words used out of context – have a grammatical term for them: interjections. Interjections are usually found at the beginning of the sentence, as we use the interjection either to get someone's attention (*"Hey! Watch out!"*) or to give ourselves time to think about the real words (*Oh, yum! This burnt, over-salted cake is utterly scrumptious!*)

## Chapter-10

# Nouns

A **noun** (Latin: *nômen*, "name") is a word that functions as the name of some specific thing or set of things, such as living creatures, objects, places, actions, qualities, states of existence, or ideas. Linguistically, a noun is a member of a large, open part of speech whose members can occur as the main word in the subject of a clause, theobject of a verb, or the object of a preposition.

Lexical categories (parts of speech) are defined in terms of the ways in which their members combine with other kinds of expressions. The syntactic rules for nouns differ from language to language. In English, nouns are those words which can occur witharticles and attributive adjectives and can function as the head of a noun phrase.

### HISTORY

Word classes (parts of speech) were described by Sanskrit grammarians from at least the 5th century BC. In Yâska's *Nirukta*, the noun (*nâma*) is one of the four main categories of words defined.

The Ancient Greek equivalent was *ónoma* (Dîîá), referred to by Plato in the *Cratylus*dialog, and later listed as one of the eight parts of speech in *The Art of Grammar*, attributed to Dionysius Thrax (2nd century BC). The term used in Latin grammar was *nômen*. All of these terms for "noun" were also words meaning "name". The English word *noun* is derived from the Latin term, through the Anglo-Norman *noun*.

The word classes were defined partly by the grammatical forms that they take. In Sanskrit, Greek and Latin, for example, nouns are categorized by gender and inflected for case and number. Because adjectives share these three grammatical categories, adjectives were originally placed in the same class as nouns. For example, in *The Art of Grammar*, words of adjectival type are largely contained in the subclass of *ónoma* described as *paragôgón* (plural *paragôgá*), meaning "derived". Similarly, the Latin *nômen* included both nouns (substantives) and adjectives, as originally did the English word *noun*, the two types being distinguished as *nouns substantive* and *nouns adjective*. (The word *nominal* is now sometimes used to denote a class that includes both nouns and adjectives.)

Many European languages use a cognate of the word *substantive* as the basic term for noun (for example, Spanish *sustantivo*, "noun"). Nouns in the dictionaries of such languages are demarked by the abbreviation *s.* or *sb.* instead of *n*, which may be used for proper nouns instead. In English, some modern authors use the word *substantive* to refer to a class that includes both nouns (single words) and noun phrases(multiword units, also called noun equivalents). It can also be used as a counterpart to *attributive* when distinguishing between a noun being used as the head (main word) of a noun phrase and a noun being used as a noun adjunct. For example, the noun *knee* can be said to be used substantively in *my knee hurts*, but attributively in *the patient needed knee replacement*.

## Definitions of nouns

Nouns have sometimes been defined in terms of the grammatical categories to which they are subject (classed by gender, inflected for case and number). Such definitions tend to be language-specific, since nouns do not have the same categories in all languages.

Nouns are frequently defined, particularly in informal contexts, in terms of their semantic properties (their meanings). Nouns are described as words that refer to a *person, place, thing, event, substance, quality, quantity*, etc. However this type of definition has been criticized by contemporary linguists as being uninformative.

There have been offered several examples of English-language nouns which do not have any reference: *drought, enjoyment, finesse, behalf*(as found in *on behalf of*), *dint* (*in dint of*), and *sake* (*for the sake of*).

Linguists often prefer to define nouns (and other lexical categories) in terms of their formal properties. These include morphologicalinformation, such as what prefixes or suffixes they take, and also their syntax – how they combine with other words and expressions of particular types. Such definitions may nonetheless still be language-specific, since syntax as well as morphology varies between languages. For example, in English it might be noted that nouns are words that can co-occur with definite articles (as stated at the start of this article), but this would not apply in Russian, which has no definite articles.

There have been several attempts, sometimes controversial, to produce a stricter definition of nouns on a semantic basis. Some of these are referenced in the Further reading section below.

## Gender

In some languages, nouns are assigned to genders, such as masculine, feminine and neuter (or other combinations). The gender of a noun (as well as its number and case, where applicable) will often entail agreement in words that modify or are related to it. For example, inFrench, the singular form of the definite article is *le* with masculine nouns and *la* with feminines; adjectives and certain verb forms also change (with the addition of *-e* with feminines). Grammatical gender often correlates with the form of the noun and the inflection pattern it follows; for example, in both Italian and Russian most nouns ending *-a* are feminine. Gender can also correlate with the sex of the noun's referent, particularly in the case of nouns denoting people (and sometimes animals). Nouns do not have gender in Modern English, although many of them denote people or animals of a specific sex.

## CLASSIFICATION OF NOUNS

### Proper nouns and common nouns

A *proper noun* or *proper name* is a noun representing unique entities (such as *Earth, India, Jupiter, Harry,* or *BMW*), as distinguished from common nouns which describe a class of entities (such as *city, animal, planet, person* or *car*).

### Countable and uncountable nouns

*Count nouns* or *countable nouns* are common nouns that can take a plural, can combine with numerals or counting quantifiers (e. g., *one, two, several, every, most*), and can take an indefinite article such as *a* or *an* (in languages which have such articles). Examples of count nouns are*chair, nose,* and *occasion.*

*Mass nouns* or *uncountable* (or *non-count*) *nouns* differ from count nouns in precisely that respect: they cannot take plurals or combine with number words or the above type of quantifiers. For example, it is not possible to refer to *a furniture* or *three furnitures*. This is true even though the pieces of furniture comprising *furniture* could be counted. Thus the distinction between mass and count nouns should not be made in terms of what sorts of things the nouns refer to, but rather in terms of how the nouns *present* these entities. Many nouns have both countable and uncountable uses; for example, *beer* is countable in "give me three beers", but uncountable in "he likes beer".

### Collective nouns

*Collective nouns* are nouns that – even when they are inflected for the singular – refer to *groups* consisting of more than one individual or entity. Examples include *committee, government,* and *police*. In English these nouns may be followed by a singular or a plural verb and referred to by a singular or plural pronoun, the singular being generally preferred when referring to the body as a unit and the plural often being preferred, especially in British English, when emphasizing the individual members. Examples of acceptable and unacceptable use given by Gowers in *Plain Words* include:

"A committee *was* appointed to consider this subject." (singular)

"The committee *were* unable to agree." (plural)

* "The committee were of one mind when I sat on them" (unacceptable use of plural)

## Concrete nouns and abstract nouns

*Concrete nouns* refer to physical entities that can, in principle at least, be observed by at least one of the senses (for instance, *chair*, *apple*, *Janet* or *atom*). *Abstract nouns,* on the other hand, refer to abstract objects; that is, ideas or concepts (such as *justice* or *hatred*). While this distinction is sometimes exclusive, some nouns have multiple senses, including both concrete and abstract ones; consider, for example, the noun *art*, which usually refers to a concept (e. g., *Art is an important element of human culture*) but which can refer to a specific artwork in certain contexts (e. g., *I put my daughter's art up on the fridge*).

Some abstract nouns developed etymologically by figurative extension from literal roots. These include *drawback, fraction, holdout,* and*uptake*. Similarly, some nouns have both abstract and concrete senses, with the latter having developed by figurative extension from the former. These include *view, filter, structure,* and *key*. In English, many abstract nouns are formed by adding noun-forming suffixes (*-ness, -ity, -ion*) to adjectives or verbs. Examples are *happiness*(from the adjective *happy*), *circulation* (from the verb *circulate*) and *serenity* (from the adjective *serene*).

## Noun phrases

A noun phrase is a phrase based on a noun, pronoun, or other noun-like word (nominal) optionally accompanied by modifiers such asdeterminers and adjectives. A noun phrase functions within a clause or sentence in a role such as that of subject, object, or complement of a verb or preposition. For example, in the sentence "The black cat sat on a dear friend of mine", the noun phrase *the black cat* serves as the subject, and the noun phrase *a dear friend of mine* serves as the complement of the preposition *on*.

## Pronouns

Nouns and noun phrases can typically be replaced by pronouns, such as *he, it, which,* and *those,* in order to avoid repetition or explicit identification, or for other reasons. For example, in the sentence *Janeth thought that he was weird,* the word *he* is a pronoun standing in place of the name of the person in question. The English word *one* can replace parts of noun phrases, and it sometimes stands in for a noun. An example is given below:

John's car is newer than *the one* that Bill has.

But *one* can also stand in for bigger sub parts of a noun phrase. For example, in the following example, *one* can stand in for *new car.* This new car is cheaper than *that one.*

## Nominalization

Nominalization is a process whereby a word that belongs to another part of speech comes to be used as a noun. In French and Spanish, for example, adjectives frequently act as nouns referring to people who have the characteristics denoted by the adjective. This sometimes happens in English as well, as in the following examples:

This legislation will have the most impact on the *poor.*

The race is not to the *swift,* nor the battle to the *strong.*

The Socialist *International* is a worldwide association of political parties.

## Nouns Definition

A **noun** is the name of a person, place, thing, or idea. Whatever exists, we assume, can be named, and that name is a noun. A **proper noun**, which names a specific person, place, or thing (Carlos, Queen Marguerite, Middle East, Jerusalem, Malaysia, Presbyterianism, God, Spanish, Buddhism, the Republican Party), is almost always capitalized. A proper noun used as an addressed person's name is called a **noun of address**. **Common nouns** name everything else, things that usually are not capitalized.

A group of related words can act as a single noun-like entity within a sentence. A **Noun Clause** contains a subject and verb and can do anything that a noun can do:

What he does for this town is a blessing.

A **Noun Phrase**, frequently a noun accompanied by modifiers, is a group of related words acting as a noun: the oil depletion allowance; the abnormal, hideously enlarged nose.

There is a separate section on word combinations that become **Compound Nouns** — such as daughter-in-law, half-moon, and stick-in-the-mud.

## Categories of Nouns

Nouns can be classified further as **count nouns**, which name anything that can be counted (four books, two continents, a few dishes, a dozen buildings); **mass nouns** (or non-count nouns), which name something that can't be counted (water, air, energy, blood); and **collective nouns**, which can take a singular form but are composed of more than one individual person or items (jury, team, class, committee, herd). We should note that some words can be either a count noun or a non-count noun depending on how they're being used in a sentence:

a. He got into trouble. (non-count)

b. He had many troubles. (countable)

c. Experience (non-count) is the best teacher.

d. We had many exciting experiences (countable) in college.

Whether these words are count or non-count will determine whether they can be used with **articles and determiners** or not. (We would not write "He got into ~~the~~ troubles," but we could write about "Thetroubles of Ireland."

Some texts will include the category of **abstract nouns**, by which we mean the kind of word that is not tangible, such as *warmth, justice, grief,* and *peace*. Abstract nouns are sometimes troublesome for non-native writers because they can appear with determiners or without: "Peace settled over the countryside." "The skirmish disrupted the peace that had settled over the countryside." See the section on **Plurals** for additional help with **collective nouns**, words that can be singular or plural, depending on context.

## Forms of Nouns

Nouns can be in the subjective, possessive, and objective case. The word *case* defines the role of the noun in the sentence. Is it a subject, an object, or does it show possession?

- The English professor [subject] is tall.
- He chose the English professor [object].
- The English professor's [possessive] car is green.

Nouns in the subject and object role are identical in form; nouns that show the possessive, however, take a different form. Usually an apostrophe is added followed by the letter *s* (except for plurals, which take the plural "-s" ending first, and then add the apostrophe). See the section on **Possessives** for help with possessive forms. There is also a **table outlining the cases of nouns and pronouns**.

Almost all nouns change form when they become **plural**, usually with the simple addition of an *-s* or *-es*. Unfortunately, it's not always that easy, and a separate section on **Plurals** offers advice on the formation of plural noun forms.

## Assaying for Nouns*

Back in the gold rush days, every little town in the American Old West had an assayer's office, a place where wild-eyed prospectors could take their bags of ore for official testing, to make sure the shiny stuff they'd found was the real thing, not "fool's gold." We offer here some assay tests for nouns. There are two kinds of tests: formal and functional — what a word looks like (the endings it takes) and how a word behaves in a sentence.

- **Formal Tests**
  1. Does the word contain a noun-making morpheme? organization, misconception, weirdness, statehood, government, democracy, philistinism, realtor, tenacity, violinist
  2. Can the word take a plural-making morpheme? pencils, boxes
  3. Can the word take a possessive-making morpheme? today's, boys'

- **Function Tests**
  4. Without modifiers, can the word directly follow an article and create a grammatical unit (subject, object, etc.)? thestate, an apple, a crate
  5. Can it fill the slot in the following sentence: "(The) _________ seem(s) all right." (or substitute other predicates such as unacceptable, short, dark, depending on the word's meaning)?

## Testing the Tests

With most nouns, the test is clear. "State," for example, can be a plural ("states"), become a possessive ("state's"), follow an article ("a/the state"), and fit in the slot ("the state seems all right"). It doesn't have a noun-making morpheme, but it passes all the other tests; it can pass as a noun. (The fact that "state" can also be a verb — "We state our case" — is not relevant.) "Greyness" cannot take plural ending nor can it be possessive, but it does contain a noun-making morphene and it can follow an article and fit in the slot sentence. Can the word "grey," which is obviously also an adjective, be a noun? It's hard to imagine it passing any of the formal tests, but it can follow an article and fill the slot: "The grey seems acceptable." And what about "running," which is often part of a verb (He is running for office)? Again, it won't pass the formal tests, but it will fit the slot sentence: "Running is all right." (It can also follow an article, but in rather an odd way: "The running is about to begin.") "Grey" and "running" are nouns, but just barely: one is an adjective acting like a noun, and the other is a verb acting like a noun (a **gerund**).

## Additional Help With Nouns

A simple exercise in **Naming Nouns** will help answer any questions you might have about count and non-count nouns and help you distinguish between plural and singular forms.

The categories of count and non-count nouns can be confusing, however, and we suggest further review, especially for writers for whom English is a second language. The second section we offer is called **Count and Non-Count**, a basic review of those concepts and their uses in sentences, with many examples. Third, we offer **WORKING WITH NOUNS**, a more extensive (and somewhat more advanced) review of the count and non-count distinction, along with exercises. Finally, just when you thought you couldn't stand such riches, we suggest you review the uses of **Articles, Determiners, and Quantifiers** with count and non-count nouns.

## What is a noun?

A noun is a part of speech that is used to name a person, place, thing, quality, or action. A noun can function as a subject, object, complement, appositive, or object of a preposition.

## Plural vs singular

Nouns can be singular or plural. The plural form of a noun is usually formed by adding s at the end of the noun. But this is not always the case. There are exceptions to the rule. Some pluralsare irregular:

| Singular | Plural |
|---|---|
| fish | fish |
| tooth | teeth |
| man | men |
| woman | women |

## Different types of nouns

There are different types of nouns:

1. An **abstract noun** names an idea, event, quality, or concept (*freedom, love, courage...*) **Concrete nouns** name something recognizable through the sense (*table, dog, house...*)
2. **Animate nouns** refer to a person, animal, or other creature (*man, elephant, chicken...*) An **inanimate noun** refers to a material object (*stone, wood, table...*)

3. **A collective noun** describes a group of things or people as a unit *(family, flock, audience...)*
4. **Common noun** is the name of a group of similar things (*table, book, window...)***Proper nouns**, however, refer to the name of a single person, place or thing *(John, Joseph, London...)*
5. **Compound nouns** refer to two or more nouns combined to form a single noun (*sister-in-law, schoolboy, fruit juice*)
6. **Countable (or count) nouns** have a singular and a plural form. In plural, these nouns can be used with a number- they can be counted. *(friends, chairs, houses, boys...)* **Uncountable (or non count) nouns**, however, can only be used in singular. They can't be counted. *(money, bread, water, coffee...)*

## Types of Nouns

There are several ways to classify the types of nouns that exist in the English language. In traditional grammar, nouns are taught to be words that refer to people, places, things, or abstract ideas. While modern linguistics find this definition to be problematic because it relies on non-specific nouns such as thing to specifically define what a noun is, much of our social understanding of what nouns are defers to the traditional definition.

## Classifications of Nouns

### *Proper Nouns*

Proper nouns are nouns that refer to specific entities. Writers of English capitalize proper nouns like *Nebraska, Steve, Harvard,* or *White House* to show their distinction from common nouns.

### *Common Nouns*

Common nouns refer to general, unspecific categories of entities. Whereas *Nebraska*is a proper noun because it signifies a specific state, the word *state* itself is a common noun because it can refer to any of the 50 states in the United States. *Harvard* refers to a particular institution of higher learning, while the common noun *university* can refer to any such institution.

### *Compound Nouns*

A compound noun contains two or more words which join together to make a single noun. Compound nouns can be words written together (closed form) such as *softball*and *toothpaste,* words that are hyphenated (hyphenated form) such as *six pack* and*son-in-law*, or separate words (open form) such as *post office* and *upper class* that go together by meaning.

### *Countable Nouns*

To linguists, these count nouns can occur in both single and plural forms, can be modified by numerals, and can co-occur with quantificational determiners like *many, most, more, several,* etc.

For example, the noun *bike* is a countable noun. Consider the following sentence:

There is a *bike* in that garage.

In this example, the word *bike* is singular as it refers to one bike that is presently residing in a particular garage.

However, *bike* can also occur in the plural form.

There are *six broken bikes* in that garage.

In this example, the noun *bikes* refers to more than one bike as it is being modified by the numeral *six*.

In addition, countable nouns can co-occur with quantificational determiners.

In that garage, *several bikes* are broken.

This sentence is grammatical, as the noun *bike* can take the modification of the quantificational determiner *several.*

Uncountable Nouns or Mass Nouns

Conversely, some nouns are not countable and are called uncountable nouns or mass nouns. For example, the word *clutter* is a mass noun.

That garage is full of *clutter*.

This sentence makes grammatical sense. However, the following example does not.

That garage is full of *clutters*.

Mass nouns can not take plural forms, and therefore a sentence containing the word*clutters* is ungrammatical.

Substances, liquids, and powders are entities that are often signified by mass nouns such as *wood, sand, water,* and *flour.* Other examples would be *milk, air, furniture, freedom, rice,* and *intelligence.*

### *Collective Nouns*

In general, collective nouns are nouns that refer to a group of something in a specific manner. Often, collective nouns are used to refer to groups of animals. Consider the following sentences.

Look at the *gaggle* of geese. There used to be *herds* of wild buffalo on the prairie. A *bevy* of swans is swimming in the pond. A *colony* of ants live in the anthill.

In the above examples, *gaggle, herds, bevy,* and *colony* are collective nouns.

### *Concrete Nouns*

Concrete nouns are nouns that can be touched, smelled, seen, felt, or tasted. *Steak, table, dog, Maria, salt,* and *wool* are all examples of concrete nouns.

Can I pet your *dog*? Please pass the *salt.* Your sweater is made of fine *wool.*

Concrete nouns can be perceived by at least one of our senses.

### *Abstract Nouns*

More ethereal, theoretical concepts use abstract nouns to refer to them. Concepts like*freedom, love, power,* and *redemption* are all examples of abstract nouns.

They *hate* us for our *freedom.* All you need is *love.* We must fight the *power.*

In these sentences, the abstract nouns refer to concepts, ideas, philosophies, and other entities that cannot be concretely perceived.

## Pronouns

Personal pronouns are types of nouns that take the place of nouns when referring to people, places or things. The personal pronouns in English are *I, you, he, she, it,* and*they*.

Amy works at a flower shop. *She* works at a flower shop.

The Greeks invented democracy. *They* invented democracy.

These pronouns take on other forms depending on what type of function they are performing in a sentence. For example, when used to signify possession of another noun, pronouns take on their possessive form such as *mine, ours, hers,* and *theirs*.

That pizza belongs to Marley. That pizza is *hers*.

When used as the object of a preposition, pronouns take on their objective case. Examples include *him, her, me, us,* and *them*.

Hand the money over to Jennifer. Hand the money over to *her*.

The police are on to John and Ray. The police are on to *them*.

Bottomline: There are nine types or classifications of nouns, each designed to serve a different purpose in a sentence.

## Common errors in the use of nouns

**Wrong:** We have decided to buy some furnitures.

**Right:** We have decided to buy some furniture.

**Wrong:** Have you received any informations?

**Right:** Have you received any information?

**Wrong:** He asked her to pack her luggages.

**Right:** He asked her to pack her luggage.

**Wrong:** The sceneries here are not good.

**Right:** The scenery here is not good.

**Wrong:** Did you hear these news?

**Right:** Did you hear this news?

### *Explanation*

Nouns like *furniture, information, advice, news, luggage* and *scenery* normally have only a singular form.

**Wrong:** Students should wear white pants.

**Right:** Students should wear white trousers.

Pants means underclothes covering the upper part of the leg.

**Wrong:** I am learning a new poetry.

**Right:** I am learning a new poem.

**Wrong:** He is my cousin brother.

**Right:** He is my cousin.

*Explanation*

*Cousin* means any child of any aunt or uncle. There is no need to say cousin brother since the noun *he* already reveals the sex of the person.

**Wrong:** One of my friend has agreed to come with me.

**Right:** One of my friends has agreed to come with me.

**Wrong:** Some of my friends has arrived.

**Right:** Some of my friends have arrived.

*Explanation*

The noun following **one of, some of, none of** and similar expressions must be plural in number, but the verb must agree with the subject in number.

Chapter-11

# Phrases

## THE GARDEN OF PHRASES

A phrase is a group of related words that does not include a subject and verb. (If the group of related words does contain a subject and verb, it is considered a **clause**.) There are several different kinds of phrases. Understanding how they are constructed and how they function within a sentence can bolster a writer's confidence in writing sentences that are sound in structure and various in form.

## NOUN PHRASE

A noun phrase comprises a **noun** (obviously) and any associated modifiers:

- The long and winding road
- A noun phrase
- any associated modifiers

The modifiers that accompany a noun can take any number of forms and combination of forms: adjectives, of course ("the tall and brilliant professor"); a participial phrase ("the road following the edge of the frozen lake"); an infinitive phrase ("the first man to walk on the moon"); a modifying clause ("the presentation that he had made the day before"); and prepositional phrases ("the building next to the lodge, over by the highway"). [See below for definitions of participial, infinitive, and prepositional phrases. ] Usually, a noun phrase will be all of a piece, all the words that compose it being contiguous with the noun itself. It is possible, however, for a noun phrase to be broken, to become what we call **discontinuous**. Sometimes part of the noun phrase is delayed until the end of the sentence so that that portion of the phrase (usually modifying phrases — participial or prepositional) can receive end weight or focus. In our first example, for instance (noun phrase in dark red),

- Several accidents have been reported involving passengers falling from trains.

we could have put the entire noun phrase together: "Several accidents involving passengers falling from trains have been reported recently." Shifting the modifying phrases of the red-colored part of the phrase to the end puts additional emphasis on that part. Here are some other examples:

- A rumor circulated among the staff that he was being promoted to Vice President. (instead of "A rumor that he was being promoted to Vice President circulated among the staff.")
- The time had come to stop spending money foolishly and to put something away for the future. (instead of "The time to stop spending money foolishly and to put something away for the future had come.")
- That hard drive was faulty that you sold me. (instead of "That hard drive that you sold me was faulty.")
- What business is it of yours? (instead of "What business of yours is it?")

Clearly, there is nothing inherently wrong with a discontinuous noun phrase. One very good reason for a discontinuous noun phrase is to achieve a balance between a subject and its predicate:

- The story is told that he was once a soldier in French Foreign Legion.

Without the discontinuous noun phrase in the sentence above, we end up with a twelve-word subject, a linking verb, and a one-word predicate — sort of lop-sided.

Authority: A Grammar of Contemporary English by Randolph Quirk, Sidney Greenbaum, Geoffrey Leech, and Jan Svartvik. Longman Group: London. 1978.

One thing you want to watch out for with noun phrases is the long compound noun phrase. * This is sometimes called the"**stacked noun phrase"** or"**packed noun phrase."** It is common to find one noun modifying another: student body, book cover, water commission. But when we create a long string of such attributive nouns or modifiers, we create difficulties:

- People who author web-pages have become aware of what is now known as the **uniform resource locator protocol problem**.

The difficulty we have here is knowing what is modifying what. Also, the reader keeps expecting the string to end, so the energy of the sentence (and our attention) dwindles into a series of false endings. Such phrases are a particular temptation in technical writing. Usually, the solution to an overly extended compound noun phrase is to take the last noun of the series and liberate it from the rest of the string (putting it at the beginning of the sentence) and then to turn at least one of the modifying nouns into a prepositional phrase:

- The problem with the protocol of uniform resource locators is now recognized by people who author web-pages as....

(This is one situation in which making a sentence longer is probably an advantage.)

A **vocative** — an addressed person's name or substitute name — is often a single word but sometimes takes the form of a noun phrase. A vocative is always treated as a parenthetical element and is thus set off from the rest of the sentence with a comma or a pair of commas (if it appears within the flow of a sentence). When vocatives are proper nouns (usually the case), they are also referred to as"**nouns of address."** Vocatives are like adverbs: they can pop up almost anywhere in the sentence. Do not, however, get into the habit of throwing commas at people's names; unless the name refers to someone who is actually being addressed, it is not a vocative and will not necessarily be parenthetical:

- He told Jorge to turn the boat around.
- Jorge, turn the boat around

Quirk and Greenbaum enumerate four different kinds of vocatives:

1. Single names, with or without a title: Jorge, Mr. Valdez, Dr. Valdez, Uncle, Grandma. Dr. Valdez, will you please address the graduates?
2. The personal pronoun *you* (not a polite form of address): **You**, put down that gun! The second person pronoun is sometimes combined with other words (but the result is often rather rude and is never used in formal prose ["You over there, hurry up!" "You with the purple hair and silver nose rings, get back in line!"]) The indefinite pronouns can also serve as a vocative: Call an ambulance, somebody! Quick, anybody! Give me a hand!
3. Appellatives (what we call people) of endearment ("Darling," "Sweetheart," "My dear," "Love") Come sit next to me, my dear.; of respect ("Sir," "Madam," "Your Honor," "Ladies and gentlemen") I would ask you, Sir, never to do that again.; of profession or status ("Professor," "Mr. President," "Madam Chairman," "Coach") Please, Coach, let me play for a while.
4. Nominal clause: Whoever is making that noise, stop it now.

Authority for this section: *A University Grammar of English* by Randolph Quirk and Sidney Greenbaum. Longman Group: Essex, England. 1993. Used with permission; examples our own.

## PREPOSITIONAL PHRASE

A prepositional phrase consists of a **preposition**, a **noun** or **pronoun** that serves as the object of the preposition, and, more often than not, an **adjective** or two that modifies the object. Ernest Hemingway apparently fell in love with the rhythms of his prepositional phrases at the beginning of his short story "Hills Like White Elephants":

The hills across the valley of the Ebro were long and white. On this side there was no shade and no trees and the station was between two lines of rails in the sun. Close against the side of the station there was the warm shadow of the buildingand a curtain, made of strings of bamboo beads, hung across the open door into the bar, to keep out flies. The American and the girl with him sat at a table in the shade, outside the building. It was very hot and the express from Barcelona would comein forty minutes. It stopped at this junction for two minutes and went on to Madrid.

Prepositional phrases usually tell when or where: "in forty minutes," "in the sun, against the side, etc." Prepositional phrases can perform other functions, however: *Except Jo*, the children were remarkably *like their father*.

A prepositional phrase at the beginning of a sentence constitutes an **introductory modifier**, which is usually a signal for a comma. However, unless an introductory prepositional phrase is unusually long, we seldom need to follow it with a comma.

You may have learned that **ending a sentence with a preposition** is a serious breach of grammatical etiquette. It doesn't take a grammarian to spot a sentence-ending preposition, so this is an easy rule to get caught up on (!). Although it is often easy to remedy the offending preposition, sometimes it isn't, and repair efforts sometimes result in a clumsy sentence. Based on shaky historical precedent, the rule itself is a latecomer to the rules of writing. Those who dislike the rule are fond of recalling Churchill's rejoinder: <"That is nonsense up with which I shall not put." We should also remember the child's complaint (attributed to E. B. White): "What did you bring that book that I don't like to be read to out of up for?"

## APPOSITIVE PHRASE

An appositive is a re-naming or amplification of a word that immediately precedes it. (An appositive, then is the opposite of anoppositive.) Frequently another kind of phrase will serve in apposition.

- My favorite teacher, **a fine chess player in her own right**, has won several state-level tournaments. [**Noun phrase** as appositive]

- The best exercise, **walking briskly**, is also the least expensive. [**Gerund phrase** as appositive]
- Tashonda's goal in life, **to become an occupational therapist**, is within her grasp this year, at last. [**Infinitive phrase** as appositive]

## ABSOLUTE PHRASE

Usually (but not always, as we shall see), an absolute phrase (also called a nominative absolute) is a group of words consisting of a**noun or pronoun** and a **participle** as well as any related **modifiers**. Absolute phrases do not directly connect to or modify any specific word in the rest of the sentence; instead, they modify the entire sentence, adding information. They are always treated as**parenthetical elements** and are set off from the rest of the sentence with a comma or a pair of commas (sometimes by a dash or pair of dashes). Notice that absolute phrases contain a **subject** (which is often modified by a participle), but not a true **finite verb**.

- **Their reputation as winners secured by victory**, the New York Liberty charged into the semifinals.
- **The season nearly finished**, Rebecca Lobo and Sophie Witherspoon emerged as true leaders.
- The two superstars signed autographs into the night, **their faces beaming happily.**

When the participle of an absolute phrase is a form of *to be*, such as *being* or *having been*, the participle is often left out but understood.

- **The season [being] over**, they were mobbed by fans in Times Square.
- **[Having been] Stars all their adult lives**, they seemed used to the attention.

Another kind of absolute phrase is found after a modified noun; it adds a focusing detail or point of focus to the idea of the main clause. This kind of absolute phrase can take the form of a prepositional phrase, an adjective phrase, or a noun phrase.

- The old firefighter stood over the smoking ruins, **his senses alert to any sign of another flare-up**.

- His subordinates, **their faces sweat-streaked and smudged with ash**, leaned heavily against the firetruck.
- They knew all too well how all their hard work could be undone — **in an instant**.

It is not unusual for the information supplied in the absolute phrase to be the most important element in the sentence. In fact, in descriptive prose, the telling details will often be wrapped into a sentence in the form of an absolute phrase:

- Coach Nykesha strolled onto the court, **her arms akimbo and a large silver whistle clenched between her teeth.**
- The new recruits stood in one corner of the gym, **their uniforms stiff and ill fitting, their faces betraying their anxiety.**

A noun phrase can also exist as an absolute phrase:

- **Your best friends**, where are they now, when you need them?
- And then there was my best friend Sally — **the dear girl** — who has certainly fallen on hard times.

It might be useful to review the material on **Misplaced Modifiers** because it is important not to confuse an absolute phrase with a misplaced modifier.

## INFINITIVE PHRASE

An infinitive phrase consists of an infinitive — the root of the verb preceded by *to* — and any modifiers or complements associated with it. Infinitive phrases can act as adjectives, adverbs, and nouns.

- Her plan **to subsidize child care** won wide acceptance among urban politicians. [modifies *plan*, functions as an adjective]
- She wanted **to raise taxes**. [noun-object of the sentence]
- **To watch Uncle Billy tell this story** is an eye-opening experience. [noun-subject of the sentence]
- To know her is **to love her**. [noun, predicate nominative]
- Juan went to college **to study veterinary medicine**. [tells us *why* he went, so it's an adverb]

### GERUND PHRASE

Gerunds, verbals that end in *-ing* and that act as nouns, frequently are associated with modifiers and complements in a gerund phrase. These phrases function as units and can do anything that a noun can do. Notice that other phrases, especially prepositional phrases, are frequently part of the gerund phrase.

- **Cramming for tests** is not a good study strategy. [gerund phrase as subject]
- John enjoyed **swimming in the lake after dark**. [gerund phrase as object]
- I'm really not interested in **studying biochemistry for the rest of my life**. [gerund phrase as object of the preposition *in* ]

### PARTICIPIAL PHRASE

Present participles, verbals ending in *-ing*, and past participles, verbals that end in *-ed* (for regular verbs) or other forms (for irregular verbs), are combined with complements and modifiers and become part of important phrasal structures. Participial phrases always act as **adjectives**. When they begin a sentence, they are often set off by a comma (as an **introductory modifier**); otherwise, participial phrases will be set off by commas if they are **parenthetical elements**.

- The stone steps, **having been worn down** by generations of students, needed to be replaced. [modifies "steps"]
- **Working around the clock**, the firefighters finally put out the last of the California brush fires. [modifies "firefighters"]
- The pond, **frozen over since early December**, is now safe for ice-skating. [modifies "pond"]

## Clauses and Phrases

*Definitions*

A **clause** is a group of words containing a subject and verb. An **independent clause** is a simple sentence. It can stand on its own.

***Examples:***

She is hungry.

*I am feeling well today.*

A **dependent clause** cannot stand on its own. It needs an independent clause to complete a sentence. Dependent clauses often begin with such words as *although, since, if, when,* and*because.*

***Examples:***

Although she is hungry ...

Whoever is hungry ...

Because I am feeling well ...

Dependent Independent

Although she is hungry, she will give him some of her food.

Whatever they decide, I will agree to.

A **phrase** is a group of words without a subject-verb component, used as a single part of speech.

***Examples:***

*Best friend* (noun phrase)

*Needing help* (adjective phrase; see the "Adjectives and Adverbs" section later in this chapter)

*With the blue shirt* (prepositional adjective phrase; see the "Prepositions" section later in this chapter)

*For twenty days* (prepositional adverb phrase)

What Is a Phrase? (with Examples)

A phrase is a group of words that stand together as a single unit, typically as part of a clause or a sentence.

A phrase does not contain a subject and verb and, consequently, cannot convey a complete thought. A phrase contrasts with a clause. A clause does contain a subject and verb, and it can convey a complete idea.

Here Are Some Examples of Phrases

Here are some examples of phrases in a well-known quote by Shirley Temple:

- I stopped believing in Santa Claus when my mother took me to see him in a department store, and he asked for my autograph. (Shirley Temple)

(This phrase acts like a noun. It is the direct object of the verb *stopped*. This phrase is a gerund phrase.)

- I stopped believing in Santa Claus when my mother took me to see him in a department store, and he asked for my autograph.

(This phrase acts like a noun. It is the subject of theadverbial clause *when my mother took me to see him in a department store*.)

- I stopped believing in Santa Claus when my mother took me to see him in a department store, and he asked formy autograph.

(This phrase acts like a noun. It is the object of the preposition *for*.)

- I stopped believing in Santa Claus when my mother took me to see him in a department store, and he asked for my autograph.

(This phrase acts like an adverb. It tells us where the activity took place. It is an adverb of place.)

The Hierarchy of Word Units

The hierarchy of word units is:

- Word (e. g., Shark)

(A word is the smallest meaningful unit.)

- Phrase (e. g., A seven-foot tiger shark)

(A phrase is a single piece of information made up of more than one word. It will not contain a subject and a verb.)

- Clause (e. g., When a seven-foot tiger shark arrived...)

(A clause is a single piece of information made up of more than one word which contains a subject and a verb.)

- Sentence (e. g., A seven-foot tiger shark arrived.)

(A sentence conveys a complete idea. It must contain at least one clause. Note: A clause that stands alone as a sentence is known as an independent clause.)

- Complex Sentence (e. g., When a seven-foot tiger shark arrived, the crew stopped fishing.)

(A complex sentence is an independent clause supported by at least one other clause.)

- Compound Sentence (e. g., A seven-foot tiger shark arrived, and the crew stopped fishing.)

(A compound sentence is a sentence made up of at least two independent clauses.)

Clause, phrase and sentence

The basic unit of English grammar is the **clause**:

[An unlucky student almost lost a 17th century violin worth almost £200, 000]

[when he left it in the waiting room of a London station. ]

[William Brown inherited the 1698 Stradivarius violin from his mother]

[and had just had it valued by a London dealer at £180, 000. ]

Clauses are made up of **phrases**:

[An unlucky student] + [almost lost] + [a 17th century violin worth almost £200, 000]

[when] + [he] + [left] + [it] + [in the waiting room of a London station. ]

[William Brown] + [inherited] + [the 1698 Stradivarius violin] + [from his mother]

[and] [had just had it valued] + [by a London dealer] + [at £180, 000. ]

We can join two or more clauses together to make **sentences**.

An unlucky student almost lost a 17th century violin worth almost £200, 000 when he left it in the waiting room of a London station.

## Phrases

In everyday speech, a **phrase** may be any group of words, often carrying a special idiomatic meaning; in this sense it is roughly synonymous with **expression**. In linguistic analysis, a phrase is a group of words (or possibly a single word) that functions as a constituent in the syntax of a sentence—a single unit within a grammatical hierarchy. A phrase appears within a clause, although it is also possible for a phrase to be a clause or to contain a clause within it.

## Common and technical use

There is a difference between the common use of the term *phrase* and its technical use in linguistics. In common usage, a phrase is usually a group of words with some special idiomatic meaning or other significance, such as "all rights reserved", "economical with the truth", "kick the bucket", and the like. It may be a euphemism, a saying or proverb, a fixed expression, a figure of speech, etc.

In grammatical analysis, particularly in theories of syntax, a phrase is any group of words, or sometimes a single word, which plays a particular role within the grammatical structure of a sentence. It does not have to have any special meaning or significance, or even exist anywhere outside of the sentence being analyzed, but it must function there as a complete grammatical unit. For example, in the sentence *Yesterday I saw an orange bird with a white neck*, the words *an orange bird with a white neck* form what is called a noun phrase, or a determiner phrasein some theories, which functions as the object of the sentence.

Theorists of syntax differ in exactly what they regard as a phrase; however, it is usually required to be a constituent of a sentence, in that it must include all the dependents of the units that it contains. This means that some expressions that may be called phrases in everyday language are not phrases in the technical sense. For example, in the sentence *I can't put up with Alex*, the words *put up with* (meaning 'tolerate') may be referred to in common language as a phrase (English expressions like this are frequently called phrasal verbs) but technically they do not form a complete phrase, since they do not include *Alex*, which is the complement of the preposition *with*.

Heads and dependents

In grammatical analysis, most phrases contain a key word that identifies the type and linguistic features of the phrase;

this is known as the head-word, or the head. The syntactic category of the head is used to name the category of the phrase; for example, a phrase whose head is a noun is called a noun phrase. The remaining words in a phrase are called the dependents of the head.

In the following phrases the head-word, or head, is bolded:

too **slowly** — Adverb phrase (AdvP); the head is an adverb

very **happy** — Adjective phrase (AP); the head is an adjective

the massive **dinosaur** — Noun phrase (NP); the head is a noun (but see below for the *determiner phrase* analysis)

**at** lunch — Preposition phrase (PP); the head is a preposition

**watch** TV — Verb phrase (VP); the head is a verb

The above five examples are the most common of phrase types; but, by the logic of heads and dependents, others can be routinely produced. For instance, the subordinator phrase:

**before** that happened — Subordinator phrase (SP); the head is a subordinating conjunction—it subordinates the independent clause

By linguistic analysis this is a group of words that qualifies as a phrase, and the head-word gives its syntactic name, "subordinator", to the grammatical category of the entire phrase. But this phrase, "**before** that happened", is more commonly classified in other grammars, including traditional English grammars, as a subordinate clause (or dependent clause); and it is then labelled *not* as a phrase, but as a clause.

Most theories of syntax view most phrases as having a head, but some non-headed phrases are acknowledged. A phrase lacking a head is known as exocentric, and phrases with heads are endocentric.

## FUNCTIONAL CATEGORIES

Some modern theories of syntax introduce certain functional categories in which the head of a phrase is some functional word or item, which may even be covert, that is, it may be a theoretical construct that need not appear explicitly in the sentence.

For example, in some theories, a phrase such as *the man* is taken to have the determiner *the* as its head, rather than the noun *man* – it is then classed as a determiner phrase (DP), rather than a noun phrase (NP). When a noun is used in a sentence without an explicit determiner, a null (covert) determiner may be posited. For full discussion, see Determiner phrase.

Another type is the inflectional phrase, where (for example) a finite verb phrase is taken to be the complement of a functional, possibly covert head (denoted INFL) which is supposed to encode the requirements for the verb to inflect – for agreement with its subject (which is thespecifier of INFL), for tense and aspect, etc. If these factors are treated separately, then more specific categories may be considered: *tense phrase* (TP), where the verb phrase is the complement of an abstract "tense" element; *aspect phrase; agreement phrase* and so on.

Further examples of such proposed categories include *topic phrase* and *focus phrase,* which are assumed to be headed by elements that encode the need for a constituent of the sentence to be marked as the topic or as the focus. See the Generative approaches section of the latter article for details.

## Phrase trees

Many theories of syntax and grammar illustrate sentence structure using phrase 'trees', which provide schematics of how the words in a sentence are grouped and relate to each other. Trees show the words, phrases, and, at times, clauses that make up sentences. Any word combination that corresponds to a complete subtree can be seen as a phrase.

There are two established and competing principles for constructing trees; they produce 'constituency' and 'dependency' trees and both are illustrated here using an example sentence. The constituency-based tree is on the left and the dependency-based tree is on the right:

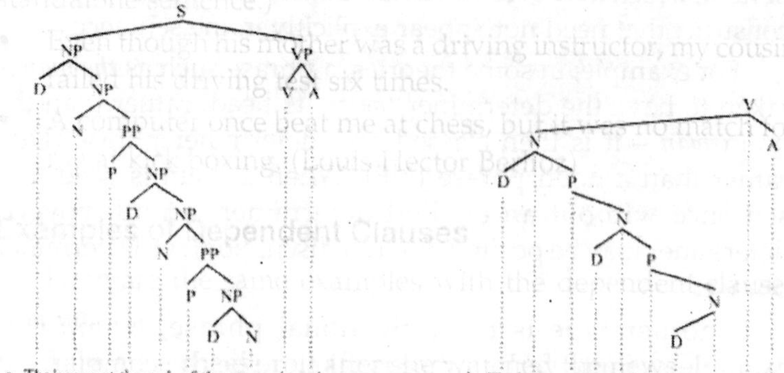

a. The house at the end of the street is red. Constituency structure

b. The house at the end of the street is red. Dependency structure

The tree on the left is of the constituency-based, phrase structure grammar, and the tree on the right is of the dependency grammar. The node labels in the two trees mark the syntactic category of the different constituents, or word elements, of the sentence.

In the constituency tree each phrase is marked by a phrasal node (NP, PP, VP); and there are eight phrases identified by phrase structure analysis in the example sentence. On the other hand, the dependency tree identifies a phrase by any node that exerts dependency upon, or dominates, another node. And, using dependency analysis, there are six phrases in the sentence.

The trees and phrase-counts demonstrate that different theories of syntax differ in the word combinations they qualify as a phrase. Here the constituency tree identifies three phrases that the dependency tree does not, namely: *house at the end of the street*, *end of the street*, and*the end*. More analysis, including about the plausibilities of both grammars, can be made empirically by applying constituency tests.

## Confusion: phrases in theories of syntax

The common use of the term "phrase" is different from that employed by some phrase structure theories of syntax. The everyday understanding of the phrase is that it consists of two or more words, whereas depending on the theory of syntax that one employs, individual words may or may not qualify as phrases. The trees in the previous section, for instance, do not view individual words as phrases. Theories of syntax that employ X-bar theory, in contrast, will acknowledge many individual words as phrases. This practice is due to the fact that sentence structure is analysed in terms of a universal schema, the X-bar schema, which sees each head as projecting at least three levels of structure: a minimal level, an intermediate level, and a maximal level. Thus an individual noun (N), such as *Susan* in *Susan laughed*, will project up to an intermediate level (N') and a maximal level (NP, noun phrase), which means that *Susan* qualifies as a phrase. (The subject slot in the sentence is required to be filled by an NP, so regardless of whether the subject is a multi-word unit like *the tall woman*, or a single word performing the same function, like *Susan*, it is called an NP in these theories.) This concept of the phrase is a source of confusion for students of syntax.

Many other theories of syntax do not employ the X-bar schema and are therefore less likely to encounter this confusion. For instance, dependency grammars do not acknowledge phrase structure in the manner associated with phrase structure grammars and therefore do not acknowledge individual words as phrases, a fact that is evident in the dependency grammar trees above and below.

## The verb phrase (VP) as a source of controversy

Most if not all theories of syntax acknowledge verb phrases (VPs), but they can diverge greatly in the types of verb phrases that they posit. Phrase structure grammars acknowledge both finite verb phrases and non-finite verb phrases as constituents. Dependency grammars, in contrast, acknowledge just non-finite verb phrases as constituents. The distinction is illustrated with the following examples:

The Republicans **may nominate Newt**. - Finite VP in bold

The Republicans may **nominate Newt**. - Non-finite VP in bold

The syntax trees of this sentence are next:

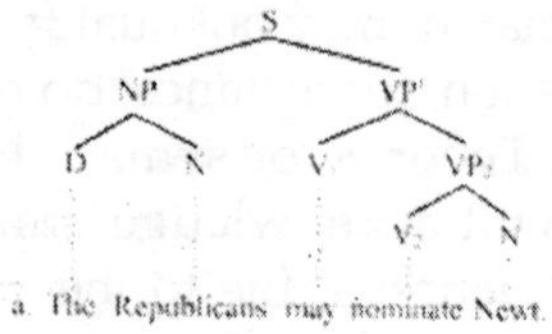


Constituency structure

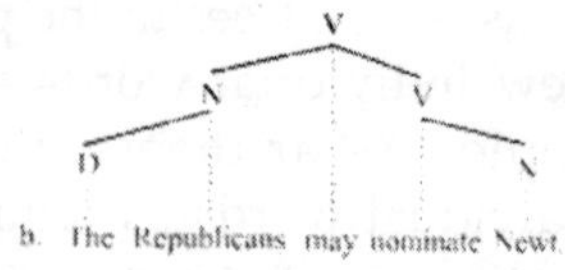


Dependency structure

The constituency tree on the left shows the finite verb string *may nominate Newt* as a phrase (= constituent); it corresponds to $VP_1$. In contrast, this same string is not shown as a phrase in the dependency tree on the right. Observe that both trees, however, take the non-finite VP string *nominate Newt* to be a phrase, since in both trees *nominate Newt* corresponds to a complete subtree.

Since there is disagreement concerning the status of finite VPs (whether they are constituents or not), empirical considerations are needed. Grammarians can (again) employ constituency tests to shed light on the controversy. Constituency tests are diagnostics for identifying the constituents of sentences and they are thus essential for identifying phrases. The results of most constituency tests do not support the existence of a finite VP constituent.

Chapter-12

# Clauses

In grammar, a **clause** is the smallest grammatical unit that can express a complete proposition. A typical clause consists of a subject and apredicate, where the predicate is typically a verb phrase–a verb together with any objects and other modifiers. However the subject is sometimes not expressed; this is often the case in null-subject languages if the subject is retrievable from context, but it also occurs in certain cases in other languages such as English (as in imperative sentences and non-finite clauses).

A simple sentence usually consists of a single finite clause with a finite verb that is independent. More complex sentences may contain multiple clauses. Main clauses (i. e. *matrix clauses, independent clauses*) are those that can stand alone as a sentence. Subordinate clauses (i. e. *embedded clauses, dependent clauses*) are those that would be awkward or incomplete alone.

## TWO MAJOR DISTINCTIONS

A primary division for the discussion of clauses is the distinction between main clauses (i. e. *matrix clauses, independent clauses*) and subordinate clauses (i. e. *embedded clauses, dependent clauses*). A main clause can stand alone, i. e. it can constitute a complete sentence by itself. A subordinate clause (i. e. *embedded clause*), in contrast, is reliant on the appearance of a main clause; it depends on the main clause and is therefore a dependent clause, whereas the main clause is an independent clause.

A second major distinction concerns the difference between finite and non-finite clauses. A finite clause contains a structurally central finite verb, whereas the structurally central word of a non-finite clause is often a non-finite verb. Traditional grammar focuses on finite clauses, the awareness of non-finite clauses having arisen much later in connection with the modern study of syntax. The discussion here also focuses on finite clauses, although some aspects of non-finite clauses are considered further below.

## Clauses according to a distinctive syntactic trait

Clauses can be classified according to a distinctive trait that is a prominent characteristic of their syntactic form. The position of the finite verb is one major trait used for classification, and the appearance of a specific type of focusing word (e. g. *wh*-word) is another. These two criteria overlap to an extent, which means that often no single aspect of syntactic form is always decisive in determining how the clause functions. There are, however, strong tendencies.

## Standard SV-clauses

Standard SV-clauses (subject-verb) are the norm in English. They are usually declarative (as opposed to exclamative, imperative, or interrogative); they express information in a neutral manner, e. g.

The pig has not yet been fed. - Declarative clause, standard SV order I've been hungry for two hours. - Declarative clause, standard SV order

... that I've been hungry for two hours. - Declarative clause, standard SV order, but functioning as a subordinate clause due to the appearance of the subordinator *that*

Declarative clauses like these are by far the most frequently occurring type of clause in any language. They can be viewed as basic, other clause types being derived from them. Standard SV-clauses can also be interrogative or exclamative, however, given the appropriate intonation contour and/or the appearance of a question word, e. g.

a. The pig has not yet been fed? - Rising intonation on *fed* makes the clause a yes/no-question.

b. The pig has not yet been fed! - Spoken forcefully, this clause is exclamative.

c. You've been hungry for how long? - Appearance of interrogative word *how* and rising intonation make the clause a constituent question

Examples like these demonstrate that how a clause functions cannot be known based entirely on a single distinctive syntactic criterion. SV-clauses are usually declarative, but intonation and/or the appearance of a question word can render them interrogative or exclamative.

## Verb first clauses

Verb first clauses in English usually play one of three roles: 1. They express a yes/no-question via subject–auxiliary inversion, 2. they express a condition as an embedded clause, or they express a command via imperative mood, e. g.

a. He **must** stop laughing. - Standard declarative SV-clause (verb second order)

b. **Should** he stop laughing? - Yes/no-question expressed by verb first order

c. **Had** he stopped laughing,... - Condition expressed by verb first order

d. **Stop** laughing! - Imperative formed with verb first order

a. They **have** done the job. - Standard declarative SV-clause (verb second order)

b. **Have** they done the job? - Yes/no-question expressed by verb first order

c. **Had** they done the job,... - Condition expressed by verb first order

d. **Do** the job! - Imperative formed with verb first order

Most verb first clauses are main clauses. Verb first conditional clauses, however, must be classified as embedded clauses because they cannot stand alone.

## *Wh*-clauses

*Wh*-clauses contain a *wh*-word. *Wh*-words often serve to help express a constituent question. They are also prevalent, though, as relative pronouns, in which case they serve to introduce a relative clause and are not part of a question. The *wh*-word focuses a particular constituent and most of the time, it appears in clause-initial position. The following examples illustrate standard interrogative *wh*-clauses. The b-sentences are direct questions (main clauses), and the c-sentences contain the corresponding indirect questions (embedded clauses):

a. Sam likes the meat. - Standard declarative SV-clause

b. **Who** likes the meat? - Matrix interrogative *wh*-clause focusing on the subject

c. They asked **who** likes the meat. - Embedded interrogative *wh*-clause focusing on the subject

a. Larry sent Susan to the store. - Standard declarative SV-clause

b. **Whom** did Larry send to the store? - Matrix interrogative *wh*-clause focusing on the object, subject-auxiliary inversion present

c. We know **whom** Larry sent to the store. - Embedded *wh*-clause focusing on the object, subject-auxiliary inversion absent

a. Larry sent Susan to the store. - Standard declarative SV-clause

b. **Where** did Larry send Susan? - Matrix interrogative *wh*-clause focusing on the oblique object, subject-auxiliary inversion present

c. Someone is wondering **where** Larry sent Susan. - Embedded *wh*-clause focusing on the oblique object, subject-auxiliary inversion absent

One important aspect of matrix *wh*-clauses is that subject-auxiliary inversion is obligatory when something other than the subject is focused. When it is the subject (or something embedded in the subject) that is focused, however, subject-auxiliary inversion does not occur.

a. **Who** called you? - Subject focused, no subject-auxiliary inversion
b. **Whom** did you call? - Object focused, subject-auxiliary inversion occurs

Another important aspect of *wh*-clauses concerns the absence of subject-auxiliary inversion in embedded clauses, as illustrated in the c-examples just produced. Subject-auxiliary inversion is obligatory in matrix clauses when something other than the subject is focused, but it never occurs in embedded clauses regardless of the constituent that is focused. A systematic distinction in word order emerges across matrix*wh*-clauses, which can have VS order, and embedded *wh*-clauses, which always maintain SV order, e. g.

a. **Why** are they doing that? - Subject-auxiliary inversion results in VS order in matrix *wh*-clause.
b. They told us **why** they are doing that. - Subject-auxiliary inversion is absent in embedded *wh*-clause.
c. *They told us **why** are they doing that. - Subject-auxiliary inversion is blocked in embedded *wh*-clause.
a. **Whom** is he trying to avoid? - Subject-auxiliary inversion results in VS order in matrix *wh*-clause.
b. We know **whom** he is trying to avoid. - Subject-auxiliary inversion is absent in embedded *wh*-clause.
c. *We know **whom** is he trying to avoid. - Subject-auxiliary inversion is blocked in embedded *wh*-clause.

## Relative clauses

Rélative clauses are a mixed group. In English they can be standard SV-clauses if they are introduced by *that* or lack a relative pronoun entirely, or they can be *wh*-clauses if they are introduced by a *wh*-word that serves as a relative pronoun.

a. 'omething happened twice. - Standard declarative SV-clause
b. something **that** happened twice - Relative clause introduced by the relative pronoun *that* and modifying the indefinite pronoun *something*
a. I know everyone. - Standard declarative SV-clause

b. everyone I know - Relative clause lacking a relative pronoun entirely and modifying the indefinite pronoun *everyone*

a. They left early - Standard declarative clause

b. the time **when** they left early - Relative clause introduced by the relative proform *when* and modifying the noun *time*

a. The woman sang a song. - Standard declarative SV-clause

b. the woman **who** sang a song. - Relative clause introduced by the relative pronoun *who* and modifying the noun *woman*

As embedded clauses, relative clauses in English cannot display subject-auxiliary inversion.

A particular type of *wh*-relative-clause is the so-called *free relative clause*. Free relatives typically function as arguments, e. g.

a. **What** he did was unexpected. - Free relative clause functioning as subject argument

b. He will flatter **whomever** is present. - Free relative clause functioning as object argument

These relative clauses are "free" because they can appear in a variety of syntactic positions; they are not limited to appearing as modifiers of nominals. The suffix *-ever* is often employed to render a standard relative pronoun as a pronoun that can introduce a free relative clause.

## Clauses according to semantic predicate-argument function

Embedded clauses can be categorized according to their syntactic function in terms of predicate-argument structures. They can function asarguments, as adjuncts, or as predicative expressions. That is, embedded clauses can be an argument of a predicate, an adjunct on a predicate, or (part of) the predicate itself. The predicate in question is usually the matrix predicate of a main clause, but embedding of predicates is also frequent.

## Argument clauses

A clause that functions as the argument of a given predicate is known as an *argument clause*. Argument clauses can appear as subjects, as objects, and as obliques. They can also modify a noun predicate, in which case they are known as *content clauses.*

That they actually helped was really appreciated. - SV-clause functioning as the subject argument

They mentioned that they had actually helped. - SV-clause functioning as the object argument

What he said was ridiculous. - *Wh*-clause functioning as the subject argument

We know **what** he said. - *Wh*-clause functioning as an object argument

He talked about **what** he had said. - *Wh*-clause functioning as an oblique object argument

The following examples illustrate argument clauses that provide the content of a noun. Such argument clauses are content clauses:

a. the claim that he was going to change it - Argument clause that provides the content of a noun (i. e. content clause)
b. the claim that he expressed - Adjunct clause (relative clause) that modifies a noun
a. the idea that we should alter the law - Argument clause that provides the content of a noun (i. e. content clause)
b. the idea that came up - Adjunct clause (relative clause) that modifies a noun

The content clauses like these in the a-sentences are arguments. Relative clauses introduced by the relative pronoun *that* as in the b-clauses here have an outward appearance that is closely similar to that of content clauses. The relative clauses are adjuncts, however, not arguments.

## Adjunct clauses

Adjunct clauses are embedded clauses that modify an entire predicate-argument structure. All clause types (SV-, verb first, *wh*-) can function as adjuncts, although the stereotypical adjunct clause is SV and introduced by a subordinator (i. e. subordinate conjunction, e. g. *after, because, before, when,* etc.), e. g.

a. Fred arrived before you did. - Adjunct clause modifying matrix clause
b. After Fred arrived, the party started. - Adjunct clause modifying matrix clause
c. Susan skipped the meal because she is fasting. - Adjunct clause modifying matrix clause

These adjunct clauses modify the entire matrix clause. Thus *before you did* in the first example modifies the matrix clause *Fred arrived*. Adjunct clauses can also modify a nominal predicate. The typical instance of this type of adjunct is a relative clause, e. g.

a. We like the music that you brought. - Relative clause functioning as an adjunct that modifies the noun *music*
b. The people **who** brought music were singing loudly. - Relative clause functioning as an adjunct that modifies the noun *people*
c. They are waiting for some food that will not come. - Relative clause functioning as an adjunct that modifies the noun *food*

Predicative clauses

An embedded clause can also function as a predicative expression. That is, it can form (part of) the predicate of a greater clause.

a. That was **when** they laughed. - Predicative SV-clause, i. e. a clause that functions as (part of) the main predicate
b. He became **what** he always wanted to be. - Predicative *wh*-clause, i. e. *wh*-clause that functions as (part of) the main predicate

These predicative clauses are functioning just like other predicative expressions, e. g. predicative adjectives (*That was good*) and predicative nominals (*That was the truth*). They form the matrix predicate together with the copula.

## Representing clauses

Some of the distinctions presented above are represented in syntax trees. These trees make the difference between main and subordinate clauses very clear, and they also illustrate well the difference between argument and adjunct clauses. The following dependency grammartrees show that embedded clauses are dependent on an element in the main clause, often on a verb:

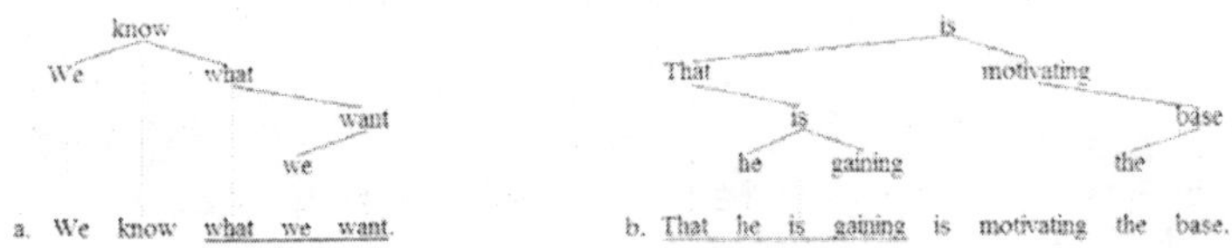


The main clause encompasses the entire tree each time, whereas the embedded clause is contained within the main clause. These two embedded clauses are arguments. The embedded *wh*-clause *what we want* is the object argument of the predicate *know*. The embedded clause *that he is gaining* is the subject argument of the predicate *is motivating*. Both of these argument clauses are directly dependent on the main verb of the matrix clause. The following trees identify adjunct clauses using an arrow dependency edge:

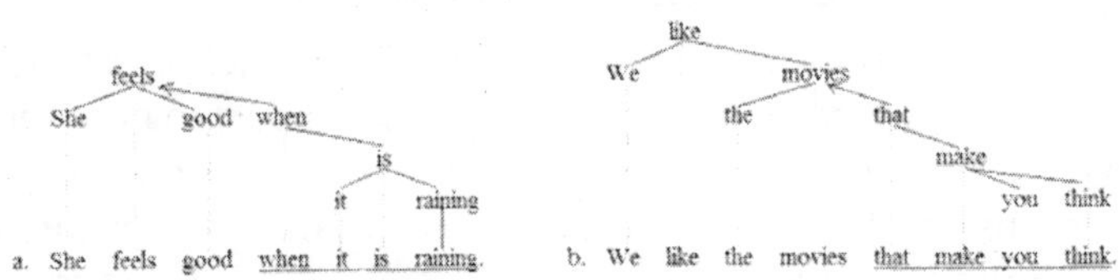


These two embedded clauses are adjunct clauses because they provide circumstantial information that modifies a superordinate expression. The first is a dependent of the main verb of the matrix clause and the second is a dependent of the object noun. The arrow dependency edges identify them as adjuncts. The arrow points away from the adjunct towards it governor to indicate that semantic selection is running counter to the direction of the syntactic dependency; the adjunct is selecting its governor. The next four trees illustrate the distinction mentioned above between matrix *wh*-clauses and embedded *wh*-clauses

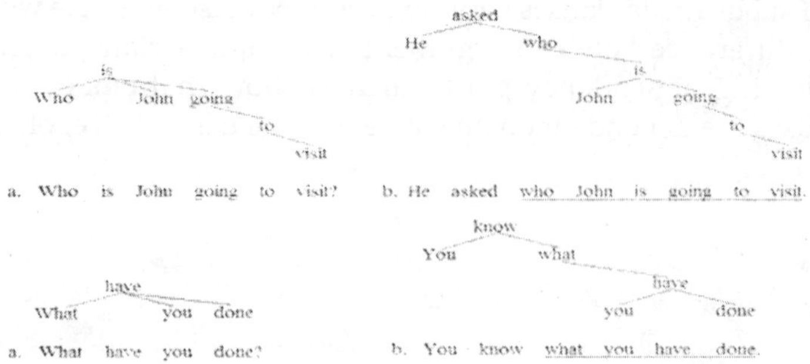


The embedded *wh*-clause is an object argument each time. The position of the *wh*-word across the matrix clauses (a-trees) and the embedded clauses (b-trees) captures the difference in word order. Matrix *wh*-clauses have V2 word order, whereas embedded wh-clauses have (what amounts to) V3 word order. In the matrix clauses, the *wh*-word is a dependent of the finite verb, whereas it is the head over the finite verb in the embedded *wh*-clauses.

## CLAUSES VS. PHRASES

There has been confusion about the distinction between clauses and phrases. This confusion is due in part to how these concepts are employed in the phrase structure grammars of the chomskyan tradition. In the 1970s, chomskyan grammars began labeling many clauses as CPs (i. e. complementizer phrases) or as IPs (i. e. inflection phrases), and then later as TPs (i. e. tense phrases), etc. The choice of labels was influenced by the theory-internal desire to use the labels consistently. The X-bar schema acknowledged at least three projection levels for every lexical head: a minimal projection (e. g. N, V, P, etc.), an intermediate projection (e. g. N′, V′, P′, etc.), and a phrase level projection (e. g. NP, VP, PP, etc.). Extending this convention to the clausal categories occurred in the interest of the consistent use of labels.

This use of labels should not, however, be confused with the actual status of the syntactic units to which the labels are attached. A more traditional understanding of clauses and phrases maintains that phrases are not clauses, and clauses are not phrases. There is a progression in the size and status of syntactic units: *words* < *phrases* < *clauses*. The characteristic trait of clauses, i. e. the presence of a subject and a (finite) verb, is absent from phrases. Clauses can be, however, embedded inside phrases.

## Non-finite clauses

The central word of a non-finite clause is usually a non-finite verb (as opposed to a finite verb). There are various types of non-finite clauses that can be acknowledged based in part on the type of non-finite verb at hand. Gerunds are widely acknowledged to constitute non-finite clauses, and some modern grammars also judge many *to*-infinitives to be the structural locus of non-finite clauses. Finally, some modern grammars also acknowledge so-called small clauses, which often lack a verb altogether. It should be apparent that non-finite clauses are (by and large) embedded clauses.

## Gerund clauses

The underlined words in the following examples are considered non-finite clauses, e. g.

a. Bill stopping the project was a big disappointment. - Non-finite gerund clause

b. Bill's stopping the project was a big disappointment. - Gerund with noun status

a. We've heard about Susan attempting a solution. - Non-finite gerund clause

b. We've heard about Susan's attempting a solution. - Gerund with noun status

a. They mentioned him cheating on the test. - Non-finite gerund clause

b. They mentioned his cheating on the test. - Gerund with noun status

Each of the gerunds in the a-sentences (*stopping*, *attempting*, and *cheating*) constitutes a non-finite clause. The subject-predicate relationship that has long been taken as the defining trait of clauses is fully present in the a-sentences. The fact that the b-sentences are also acceptable illustrates the enigmatic behavior of gerunds. They seem to straddle two syntactic categories: they can function as non-finite verbs or as nouns. When they function as nouns as in the b-sentences, it is debatable whether they constitute clauses, since nouns are not generally taken to be constitutive of clauses.

## *to*-infinitive clauses

Some modern theories of syntax take many *to*-infinitives to be constitutive of non-finite clauses. This stance is supported by the clear predicate status of many *to*-infinitives. It is challenged, however, by the fact that *to*-infinitives do not take an overt subject, e. g.

a. She refuses to consider the issue.

a. He attempted to explain his concerns.

The *to*-infinitives *to consider* and *to explain* clearly qualify as predicates (because they can be negated). They do not, however, take overt subjects. The subjects *she* and *he* are dependents of the matrix verbs *refuses* and *attempted*, respectively, not of the *to*-infinitives. Data like these are often addressed in terms of control. The matrix predicates *refuses* and *attempted* are control verbs; they control the embedded predicates *consider* and *explain*, which means they determine which of their arguments serves as the subject argument of the embedded predicate. Some theories of syntax posit the null subject PRO (i. e. pronoun) to help address the facts of control constructions, e. g.

b. She refuses PRO to consider the issue.

b. He attempted PRO to explain his concerns.

With the presence of PRO as a null subject, *to*-infinitives can be construed as complete clauses, since both subject and predicate are present.

One must keep in mind, though, that PRO-theory is particular to one tradition in the study of syntax and grammar (Government and Binding Theory, Minimalist Program). Other theories of syntax and grammar (e. g. Head-Driven Phrase

Structure Grammar, Construction Grammar, dependency grammar) reject the presence of null elements such as PRO, which means they are likely to reject the stance that *to*-infinitives constitute clauses.

## Small clauses

Another type of construction that some schools of syntax and grammar view as non-finite clauses is the so-called small clause. A typical small clause consists of a noun phrase and a predicative expression, e. g. We consider that a joke. - Small clause with the predicative noun phrase *a joke* Something made him angry. - Small clause with the predicative adjective *angry*

She wants us to stay. - Small clause with the predicative non-finite *to*-infinitive *to stay* The subject-predicate relationship is clearly present in the underlined strings. The expression on the right is a predication over the noun phrase immediately to its left. While the subject-predicate relationship is indisputably present, the underlined strings do not behave as singleconstituents, a fact that undermines their status as clauses. Hence one can debate whether the underlined strings in these examples should qualify as clauses. The layered structures of the chomskyan tradition are again likely to view the underlined strings as clauses, whereas the schools of syntax that posit flatter structures are likely to reject clause status for them.

## What Are Clauses? (with Examples)

A clause is a group of words that includes a subject and averb. A clause can be distinguished from a phrase, which does not contain a subject and a verb (e. g., *in the afternoon, drinking from the bowl*).

An independent clause can express a complete thought (and can be a standalone sentence). A dependent clause is usually a supporting part of a sentence, and it cannot stand by itself as a meaningful proposition (idea).

## Examples of Independent Clauses

Here are some examples of independent clauses (shaded):

- Tara ate a cheese roll after she watched the news.

(*Tara ate a cheese roll* is an independent clause. It works as a standalone sentence.)

- Even though his mother was a driving instructor, my cousin failed his driving test six times.
- A computer once beat me at chess, but it was no match for me at kick boxing. (Louis Hector Berlioz)

## Examples of Dependent Clauses

Here are the same examples with the dependent clauses shaded:

- Tara ate a cheese roll after she watched the news.

(The clause *after she watched the news* is a dependent clause. It does not work as a standalone sentence.)

- Even though his mother was a driving instructor, my cousin failed his driving test six times.
- A computer once beat me at chess, but it was no match for me at kick boxing.

These three dependent clauses (or subordinate clauses as they're also called) could have been independent clauses. However, the opening word(s) (in these examples *after*, *Even though*, and *but*) turned them into dependent clauses. The opening words are known as dependent words, the main type of which is subordinating conjunctions.

## How Are Clauses Used in Sentences?

Clauses can play a variety of roles in sentences. A clause can act as a noun, an adjective, or an adverb.

Noun Clauses

- I cannot remember what I said last night.

(In this example, the clause acts like a noun.)

Compare the example above to this:

- I cannot remember **my speech**.

(*speech* = noun)

Read more about noun clauses.

## ADJECTIVE CLAUSES

- My dog, who usually refuses to go near the water, dived in the canal to chase a water vole.

  (In this example, the clause acts like an adjective.)

  Compare the example above to this:

- My **water-shy** dog dived in the canal to chase a water vole.

  (*water-shy* = adjective)

  Read more about adjective clauses.

If an adjective clause could be removed without wrecking the sentence (i. e., it just adds additional information), then it should be offset with commas. (You could equally use brackets or dashes.) A clause which can be safely removed is called a non-restrictive clause. A restrictive clause, on the other hand, is one which cannot be removed because it's essential to the sentence. Restrictive clauses are not offset with commas. For example:

- The man who lives next door is getting ruder.

(This is an example of a restrictive clause. You cannot remove it. There are no commas.)

- Councillor Simon Smith, who lives next door, is getting ruder.

(This is an example of a non-restrictive clause. You can remove it. It's just additional information. That's why there are commas around it.)

Read more about using commas with *which* and *who*.

Adverbial Clauses

- He lost his double chin after he gave up beer.

  (In this example, the clause acts like an adverb.)

  Compare the example above to this:

### Relative Clauses: Common Errors

#### *The First Problem: To Comma or not to Comma*

Relative clauses are not always set off by commas in English. The trick to deciding when a comma is necessary is to decide whether the information in the relative clause is "necessary" or "extra."

"Necessary" means that the information in the relative clause is necessary to understand the basic meaning of the sentence. "Extra" means the relative clause provides extra information which is not necessary to understand the sentence.

**Necessary = no comma**

Extra = comma

The people who live next door have a poodle.

Without the relative clause it is unclear which people you mean. Thus, the information in the relative clause is necessary and there is no comma.

The Hills, who live next door, have a poodle. It is already clear which people are being talked about; the fact that they live next door is an extra detail. Thus, information in the relative clause is extra and there is a comma.

Be aware that the question of "necessary" vs. "extra" is a question of what you mean in the sentence. It is not always a simple question of what is grammatically correct - it could be that you could write the same sentence with and without commas and both would be grammatically correct, but they would have different meanings.

Her husband who lives in California is a lawyer.

Because there are no commas around this relative clause, it means that it provides information necessary to understand the sentence - in other words, she has multiple husbands and you have to specify that you mean the one in California.

Her husband, who lives in California, is a lawyer. Unless she is a polygamist, this is the correct punctuation.

## The Second Problem: Choosing the Relative Pronoun

*Who / whom* is used when you are referring to people, groups of people, and animals (especially pets).

*Which* and *that* are used for things.

*Which* is used to introduce both "necessary" and "extra" relative clauses. *That* is only used to introduce "necessary" relative clauses, and thus is NOT set off by commas.

Chapter-13

# Tenses

## GRAMMATICAL TENSE

In grammar, **tense** is a category that expresses time reference. Tenses are usually manifested by the use of specific forms of verbs, particularly in their conjugation patterns.

Basic tenses found in many languages include the past, present and future. Some languages have only two distinct tenses, such as past and non-past, or future and non-future. There are also tenseless languages, like Chinese, which do not have tense at all. On the other hand, some languages make finer tense distinctions, such as remote vs. recent past, or near vs. remote future.

Tenses generally express time relative to the moment of speaking. In some contexts, however, their meaning may be relativised to a point in the past or future which is established in the discourse (the moment being spoken about). This is called *relative* (as opposed to *absolute*) tense. Some languages have different verb forms or constructions which manifest relative tense, such as pluperfect ("past-in-the-past") and "future-in-the-past".

Expressions of tense are often closely connected with expressions of the category of aspect; sometimes what are traditionally called tenses (in languages such as Latin) may in modern analysis be regarded as combinations of tense with aspect. Verbs are also often conjugated formood, and since in many cases the three categories are not manifested separately, some languages may be described in terms of a combinedtense–aspect–mood (TAM) system.

## Etymology

The English noun *tense* comes from Old French *tens*"time" (spelled *temps* in modern French through deliberate archaisation), from Latin*tempus*"time". It is not related to the adjective *tense*, which comes from Latin *tensus*, the perfect passive participle of *tendere*"stretch".

## Uses of the term

In modern linguistic theory, tense is understood as a category that expresses (grammaticalises) time reference; namely one which, usinggrammatical means, places a state or action in time. Nonetheless, in many descriptions of languages, particularly in traditional European grammar, the term "tense" is applied to series of verb forms or constructions that express not merely position in time, but also additional properties of the state or action – particularly aspectual or modal properties.

The category of aspect expresses how a state or action relates to time – whether it is seen as a complete event, an ongoing or repeated situation, etc. Many languages make a distinction between perfective aspect (denoting complete events) and imperfective aspect (denoting ongoing or repeated situations); some also have other aspects, such as a perfect aspect, denoting a state following a prior event. Some of the traditional "tenses" express time reference together with aspectual information. In Latin and French, for example, the imperfect denotes past time in combination with imperfective aspect, while other verb forms (the Latin perfect, and the French *passé composé* or *passé simple*) are used for past time reference with perfective aspect.

The category of mood is used to express modality, which includes such properties as uncertainty, evidentiality, and obligation. Commonly encountered moods include the indicative, subjunctive, and conditional. Mood can be bound up with tense, aspect, or both, in particular verb forms. Hence certain languages are sometimes analysed as having a single tense–aspect–mood (TAM) system, without separate manifestation of the three categories.

The term *tense*, then, particularly in less formal contexts, is sometimes used to denote any combination of tense proper, aspect, and mood. As regards English, there are many verb forms and constructions which combine time reference with continuous and/or perfect aspect, and with indicative, subjunctive or conditional mood. Particularly in some English language teaching materials, some or all of these forms can be referred to simply as tenses.

Particular tense forms need not always carry their basic time-referential meaning in every case. A present tense form may sometimes refer to the past (as in the historical present), a past tense form may sometimes refer to the non-past (as in some English conditional sentences), and so on.

## Possible tenses

Not all languages have tense: tenseless languages include Burmese, Chinese and Dyirbal. Some languages have all three basic tenses (thepast, present and future), while others have only two: some have past and non-past tenses, the latter covering both present and future times (as in Japanese, and in English in some analyses), whereas others such as Greenlandic and Quechua have future and non-future. Some languages have four or more tenses, making finer distinctions either in the past (e. g. remote vs. recent past) or in the future (e. g. near vs. remote future). The six-tense language Kalaw Lagaw Ya of Australia has the remote past, the recent past, the today past, the present, the today/near future and the remote future.

A historical past tense, used for events perceived as historical, is found in, for example, the Amazonian Cubeo language.

Tenses that refer specifically to "today" are called hodiernal tenses; these can be either past or future. Apart from Kalaw Lagaw Ya, another language which features such tenses is Mwera, a Bantu language of Tanzania. It is also suggested that in 17th-century French, the *passé composé* served as a hodiernal past. Tenses which contrast with hodiernals, by referring to the past before today or the future after today, are called pre-hodiernal and post-hodiernal respectively. Some languages also have a crastinal tense, a future tense referring specifically to tomorrow (found in some Bantu languages); or a hesternal tense, a past tense referring spefically to yesterday (although this name is also sometimes used to mean pre-hodiernal). A tense for after tomorrow is thus called post-crastinal, and one for before yesterday is called pre-hesternal.

Another tense found in some languages, including Luganda, is the *still tense*, used to indicate that a state or ongoing action is still the case (or, in the negative, is no longer the case). Luganda also has tenses meaning "so far" and "not yet".

Some languages have special tense forms that are used to express relative tense. Tenses that refer to the past relative to the time under consideration are called *anterior*; these include the pluperfect (for the past relative to a past time) and the future perfect (for the past relative to a future time). Similarly, *posterior* tenses refer to the future relative to the time under consideration, as with the English "future-in-the-past":*(he said that) he **would go***. Relative tense forms are also sometimes analysed as combinations of tense with aspect: the perfect aspect in the anterior case, or the prospective aspect in the posterior case.

## Tense marking

Tense is normally indicated by the use of a particular verb form – either an inflected form of the main verb, or a multi-word construction, or both in combination. Inflection may involve the use of affixes, such as the *-ed* ending that marks the past tense of English regular verbs, but can also entail stem modifications, such as ablaut, as found in the strong verbs in English and other Germanic languages, or reduplication. Multi-word tense constructions often involve auxiliary verbs or clitics. Examples which combine both types of tense marking include the French*passé composé*, which has an auxiliary verb together with the inflected past participle form of the main verb; and the Irish past tense, where the proclitic *do* (in various surface forms) appears in conjunction with the affixed or ablaut-modified past tense form of the main verb.

As has already been mentioned, indications of tense are often bound up with indications of other verbal categories, such as aspect and mood. The conjugation patterns of verbs often also reflect agreement with categories pertaining to the subject, such as person, number and gender. It is consequently not always possible to identify elements that mark any specific category, such as tense, separately from the others.

A few languages have been shown to mark tense information (as well as aspect and mood) on nouns. This may be called nominal TAM.

Languages that do not have grammatical tense, such as Chinese, express time reference chiefly by lexical means – through adverbials, time phrases, and so on. (The same is done in tensed languages, to supplement or reinforce the time information conveyed by the choice of tense.) Time information is also sometimes conveyed as a secondary feature by markers of other categories, as with the Chinese aspect markers *le* and *guo*, which in most cases place an action in past time. However, much time information is conveyed implicitly by context – it is therefore not always necessary, when translating from a tensed to a tenseless language, say, to express explicitly in the target language all of the information conveyed by the tenses in the source.

## In particular languages

### *Latin and Ancient Greek*

Latin is traditionally described as having six tenses (the Latin for "tense" being *tempus*, plural *tempora*):

- Present *(praesens)*
- Imperfect *(praeteritum imperfectum)*
- Perfect *(praeteritum perfectum)*
- Future *(futurus)*
- Pluperfect *(plus quam perfectum)*
- Future perfect *(anterior futurus)*

Of these, the imperfect and perfect can be considered to represent a past tense combined with imperfective and perfective aspect respectively (the first is used for habitual or ongoing past actions or states, and the second for completed actions). The pluperfect and future perfect arerelative tenses, referring to the past relative to a past time or relative to a future time.

Latin verbs are conjugated for tense (and aspect) together with mood (indicative, subjunctive, and sometimes imperative) and voice (active or passive). Most forms are produced by inflecting the verb stem, with endings that also depend on the person and number of the subject. Some of the passive forms are produced using a participle together with a conjugated auxiliary verb. For details of the forms, see Latin conjugation.

The tenses of Ancient Greek are similar, but with a three-way aspect contrast in the past: the aorist, the perfect and the imperfect. The aorist was the "simple past", while the imperfective denoted uncompleted action in the past, and the perfect was used for past events having relevance to the present.

The study of modern languages has been greatly influenced by the grammar of the Classical languages, since early grammarians, often monks, had no other reference point to describe their language. Latin terminology is often used to describe modern languages, sometimes with a change of meaning, as with the application of "perfect" to forms in English that do not necessarily have perfective meaning, or the words *Imperfekt* and *Perfekt* to German past tense forms that mostly lack any relationship to the aspects implied by those terms.

### *English*

English has only two morphological tenses: the present, as in *he* ***goes***, and the past, as in *he* ***went***. The present tense sometimes references the future (as in *the bus* ***leaves*** *tomorrow*), and thus may also be called the non-past (or present–future) tense. (It also sometimes references the past, however, in what is called the historical present.)

Constructions with the modal auxiliary verbs *will* and *shall* also frequently reference the future (although they have other uses as well); these are often described as the English future tense. Less commonly, forms with the auxiliaries *would* and (rarely) *should* are described as arelative tense, the future-in-the-past. (The same forms are used for the conditional mood, and for various other meanings.)

The present and past are distinguished by verb form, using either ablaut (*sing(s)* ~ *sang*) or suffix (*walk(s)* ~ *walked*). For details, see English verbs.

English also has continuous (progressive) aspect and perfect aspect; these together produce four aspectual types: simple, continuous, perfect, and perfect continuous. Each of these can combine with the tenses to produce a large set of different constructions, mostly involving one or more auxiliary verbs together with a participle or infinitive:

| | | Tenses | | | |
|---|---|---|---|---|---|
| | | Morphological | | With auxiliaries | |
| | | Present (non-past) | Past | Future | Future-in-the-past |
| Aspects | Simple | *go(es)* | *went* | *will go* | *would go* |
| | Continuous | *am/is/are going* | *was/were going* | *will be going* | *would be going* |
| | Perfect | *have/has gone* | *had gone* | *will have gone* | *would have gone* |
| | Perfect continuous | *have/has been going* | *had been going* | *will have been going* | *would have been going* |

In some contexts, particularly in English language teaching, the tense–aspect combinations in the above table may be referred to simply as tenses. For details of the uses of these constructions, as well as additional verb forms representing different grammatical moods, see Uses of English verb forms.

## Other Indo-European languages

Proto-Indo-European verbs had present, perfect (stative), imperfect and aorist forms – these can be considered as representing two tenses (present and past) with different aspects. Most languages in the Indo-European family have developed systems either with two morphological tenses (present or "non-past", and past) or with three (present, past and future). The tenses often form part of entangled tense–aspect–moodconjugation systems. Additional tenses, tense–aspect combinations, etc. can be provided by compound constructions containing auxiliary verbs.

The Germanic languages (which include English) have present (non-past) and past tenses formed morphologically, with future and other additional forms made using auxiliaries. In standard German, the compound past *(Perfekt)* has replaced the simple morphological past in most contexts.

The Romance languages (descendants of Latin) have past, present and future morphological tenses, with additional aspectual distinction in the past. French is an example of a language where, as in German, the simple morphological perfective past *(passé simple)* has mostly given way to a compound form *(passé composé)*.

Irish, a Celtic language, has past, present and future tenses. The past contrasts perfective and imperfective aspect, and some verbs retain such a contrast in the present. Classical Irish had a three-way aspectual contrast of simple–perfective–imperfective in the past and present tenses.

Persian, an Indo-Iranian language, has past and non-past forms, with additional aspectual distinctions. Future can be expressed using an auxiliary.

In the Slavic languages, verbs are intrinsically perfective or imperfective. In Russian and some other languages in the group, perfective verbs have past and future tenses, while imperfective verbs have past, present and future, the imperfective future being a compound tense in most cases. The future tense of perfective verbs is formed in the same way as the present tense of imperfective verbs. However, in South Slavic languages, there may be a greater variety of forms – Bulgarian, for example, has present, past (both "imperfect" and "aorist") and future tenses, for both perfective and imperfective verbs, as well as perfect forms made with an auxiliary.

### Other languages

Finnish and Hungarian, both members of the Uralic language family, have morphological present (non-past) and past tenses. The Hungarian verb *van* ("to be") also has a future form. Turkish verbs conjugate for past, present and future, with a variety of aspects and moods.

Arabic verbs have past and non-past; future can be indicated by a prefix.

Korean verbs have a variety of affixed forms which can be described as representing present, past and future tenses, although they can alternatively be considered to be aspectual. Similarly, Japanese verbs are described as having present and past tenses, although they may be analysed as aspects. Chinese and many other East Asian languages generally lack inflection and are considered to be tenseless languages, although they may have aspect markers which convey certain information about time reference.

For examples of languages with a greater variety of tenses, see the section on possible tenses, above. Fuller information on tense formation and usage in particular languages can be found in the articles on those languages and their grammars.

## SEQUENCE OF TENSES

**Sequence of tenses** (known in Latin as ***consecutio temporum***, and also known as **agreement of tenses, succession of tenses** and**tense harmony**) is a set of grammatical rules of a particular language, governing the agreement between the tenses of verbs in relatedclauses or sentences.

A typical context in which rules of sequence of tenses apply is that of indirect speech. If, at some past time, someone spoke a sentence in a particular tense (say the present tense), and that act of speaking is now being reported, the tense used in the clause that corresponds to the words spoken may or may not be the same as the tense that was used by the original speaker. In some languages the tense tends to be "shifted back", so that what was originally spoken in the present tense is reported using the past tense (since what was in the present at the time of the original sentence is in the past relative to the time of reporting). English is one of the languages in which this often occurs. For example, if someone said "I **need** a drink", this may be reported in the form "She said she **needed** a drink", with the tense of the verb *need*changed from present to past.

The "shifting back" of tense as described in the previous paragraph may be called **backshifting** or an **attracted sequence** of tenses. In languages and contexts where such a shift does not occur, there may be said by contrast to be a **natural sequence**.

## English

In English, an *attracted sequence* of tenses (backshifting) is often used in indirect speech and similar contexts. The attracted sequence can be summarized as follows: If the main verb of a sentence is in the past tense, then other verbs must also express a past viewpoint, except when a general truth is being expressed.

For example, if Batman spoke the following words:

I **need** a special key for the Batmobile.

the speech act may be reported using the following words:

Batman **said** that he **needed** a special key for the Batmobile.

with the present tense *need* replaced by the past tense *needed*, since the main verb of saying (*said*) is in the past tense. Further examples can be found at Uses of English verb forms: Indirect speech.

In some cases, though, a *natural sequence* of tenses is more appropriate. Here the tense of a verb in a subordinate clause is not determined by the tense of the verb in the superordinate clause, but is determined simply according to the sense of the clause taken apart from the rest of the sentence. The rule for writers following the natural sequence of tenses can be expressed as follows: imagine yourself at the point in time denoted by the main verb, and use the tense for the subordinate verb that you would have used *at that time*. Thus the tense used in the indirect speech remains the same as it was in the words as originally spoken. This is normal when the main verb is in the present or future tense (as opposed to past tense or conditional mood). For example:

Batman **says** that he **needs** a special key for the Batmobile. (main verb in present tense) Batman **has said** that he **needs** a special key for the Batmobile. (main verb in present perfect, not past tense, so no backshifting)

However it is also possible to use the natural sequence even if the main verb is past or conditional:

Batman **said** that he **needs** a special key for the Batmobile.

This option is more likely to be used when the circumstance being expressed remains equally true now as it did when the speech act took place, and especially if the person reporting the words agrees that they are true or valid.

Debate amongst grammarians over the appropriateness of the two types of sequence of tenses goes back as far as the 18th century. Use of the attracted sequence sometimes leads to additional problems when the grammatical construction of indirect speech includes an incorporated quotation – that is, when an attempt is made (though using indirect rather than direct speech) to report the words actually spoken. For example, if a minister spoke the words "Such a policy is not without its drawbacks", then a writer may attempt to report this as follows:

The minister admitted that "such a policy is not without its drawbacks". using quotation marks to denote that that portion of the sentence represents the minister's actual words. This, however, requires use of the natural sequence of tenses, which might not be felt appropriate in the given situation. There are various possible solutions to this problem:

- Rearrange the sentence so that the incorporated quotations become set off, possibly as direct speech:

The minister did not claim perfection: "such a policy is not without its drawbacks", he admitted.

- Cut down the incorporated quotation to exclude the verb:

The minister admitted that such a policy was "not without its drawbacks".

- Use square brackets to indicate where the words deviate from those actually spoken:

The minister admitted that "such a policy [was] not without its drawbacks".

Similar problems arise from the other changes that typically occur in indirect speech, such as changes of pronoun (depending on speaker), etc.

For more details, see the article on indirect speech, and also the article on uses of English verb forms, particularly the sections on indirect speech and dependent clauses.

## Russian

Indirect speech in Russian and other Slavic languages generally uses the natural sequence of tenses (there is no backshifting). For examples, see Indirect speech: Russian.

Common errors in the use of tenses

- Incorrect: It is raining for two days.
- Correct: It **has been raining** for two days.
- Incorrect: The baby is sleeping for three hours now.
- Correct: The baby **has been sleeping** for three hours now.

Here the error lies in using the present continuous instead of the present perfect continuous. We use the present perfect continuous tense to talk about an action which started in the past, has gone on till the present and is still continuing.

- Incorrect: I have seen him yesterday.
- Correct: I **saw** him yesterday.
- Incorrect: He has returned from London last week.
- Correct: He **returned** from London last week.

Here the error lies in using the present perfect tense instead of the simple past tense. The present perfect is a present tense. It can't be used with adverbs of past time.

- Incorrect: See that you will not do any damage.
- Correct: See that you **do not** do any damage.

It is wrong to use the future tense in the subordinate clause when the verb in the main clause is in the imperative mood.

- Incorrect: I will call you when the dinner will be ready.
- Correct: I will call you when the dinner **is**ready.
- Incorrect: He will help if you will ask him.
- Correct: He will help if you **ask** him.

When the verb in the main clause is in the future tense, the verb in the subordinate clause should be in the present and not in the future.

# Bibliography


- Brown Corpus and Lancaster-Oslo-Bergen Corpus, quoted in Peters (2004: 1)
- Comrie 1985, pp. 50-53.
- Daniel Nettle, *The Fyem Language of Northern Nigeria*, LINCOM Europa 1998
- Díaz Collazos, Ana María. https://www. academia. edu/ 6254347/Spanish_indefinite_articles_in_the_Nikkei_as_ Colombian-Japanese_community
- Earl W. Stevick, *Adapting and writing language lessons*, U. S. Foreign Service Institute, 1971, p. 302.
- Fabricius-Hansen, "Tense", in the *Encyclopedia of Language and Linguistics*, 2nd ed., 2006
- From the United States Declaration of Independence (1776).
- Gee, James Paul (1974)."*Get Passive": On Some Constructions with "get"*. Indiana University Linguistics Club.
- Genetic Linguistics
- Geoffrey K. Pullum."The passive in English". *Language Log*.
- Harper, Douglas."tense". *Online Etymology Dictionary*.
- International Studies Review (10 March 2010)."Journal house style points" (PDF). Retrieved 2010-08-05.
- Joan Bybee, Revere Perkins, William Pagliuca, *The Evolution of Grammar: Tense, Aspect, and Modality in the Languages of the World*, University of Chicago Press, 1994, p. 101.
- Lawrence, Erma (1977). *Haida dictionary*. Fairbanks: Alaska Native Language Center. p. 64.

- Mark Liberman, "'Passive Voice' — 1397-2009 — R. I. P.," in Language Log, 2009 March 12.
- Mark Liberman, "The aggrieved passive voice," in Language Log, 2009 March 16.
- *Merriam-Webster's Dictionary of English Usage*. Merriam-Webster. 1994. pp. 720–721. ISBN 978-0-87779-132-4. Retrieved 27 January2013.
- Nancy Franklin, "The Dolor of Money," *The New Yorker*, 2009 March 23, at 24, 25.
- Nancy L. Morse, Michael B. Maxwell, *Cubeo Grammar*, Summer Institute of Linguistics, 1999, p. 45.
- Nature Publishing Group (2010). Writing for a Nature journal "How to write a paper". *Authors & referees*. Retrieved 2010-08-05.
- Peters, Pam (2004). *The Cambridge Guide to English Usage*. Cambridge University Press. p. 411. ISBN 0-521-62181-X.
- Recasens, Taulé and Martíhttp://www. researchgate. net/ publication/228748115_First-mention_definites_more_than_exceptional_cases
- ScienceDirect Master, Peter (1997) "The English Article System: acquisition, function, and pedagogy" in: *System*, Volume 25, Issue 2, pp. 215–232
- See e. g. Tony Penston, *A Concise Grammar for English Language Teachers*, TP Publications, 2005, p. 17.
- tempus. Charlton T. Lewis and Charles Short. *A Latin Dictionary* on Perseus Project.
- The 500 Most Commonly Used Words in the English Language. World English. Archived from the original on 13 January 2007. Retrieved 2007-01-14.
- *The American Heritage Book of English Usage* (1996).
- The Use and Non-Use of Articles.